PUB W
AROU
Birmingham and Coventry

THIRTY CIRCULAR WALKS
AROUND BIRMINGHAM AND COVENTRY INNS

Richard Shurey

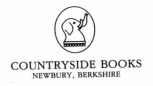

COUNTRYSIDE BOOKS
NEWBURY, BERKSHIRE

First Published 1995
© Richard Shurey 1995

COUNTRYSIDE BOOKS
3 Catherine Road
Newbury, Berkshire

ISBN 1 85306 370 3

Designed by Mon Mohan
Cover illustration by Colin Doggett
Photographs and maps by the author

Produced through MRM Associates Ltd., Reading
Typeset by Paragon Typesetters, Queensferry, Clwyd
Printed in England by J. W. Arrowsmith Ltd., Bristol

Contents

Publisher's Note

We hope that you obtain considerable enjoyment from this book; great care has been taken in its preparation. However, changes of landlord and actual closures are sadly not uncommon. Likewise, although at the time of publication all routes followed public rights of way or permitted paths, diversion orders can be made and permissions withdrawn.

We cannot of course be held responsible for such diversion orders and any inaccuracies in the text which result from these or any other changes to the routes nor any damage which might result from walkers trespassing on private property. However, we are anxious that all details covering the walks and the pubs are kept up to date and would therefore welcome information from readers which would be relevant to future editions.

Introduction

The huge conurbations of Birmingham and Coventry are surrounded by delightful and varied countryside where there are many pretty villages. A proper mix in an English village includes the school, the shop, the church and the pub. Fortunately, while other features are disappearing from the rural scene, the pub, albeit in declining numbers, is surviving.

One of the most charming aspects of our hostelries (which are the envy of travellers in other lands) is their infinite variety. Even when owned and managed as part of a nationwide chain, each place has its own unique character. Many of the pubs mentioned in this book have been places of refreshment for centuries; they probably served either the stage-coach traffic or the farm labourers and villagers. Today the welcome will be just as warm but the clientele will be different – and among them will be walkers who come from the towns for country air and pleasant exercise as an antidote to the pressures of everyday life.

I have tried to include a good mix of pubs but I was sometimes inhibited because a good inn was not in an area conducive to a ramble. The landlords were, without exception, enthusiastic about the project. Although most pubs have large car parks it is a common courtesy to confirm with the landlord that the vehicle can be left during the time of the ramble.

There has been a revolution in pub food over the last few decades. Whereas formerly one was fortunate to find sandwiches and crisps on offer, today the array of food is daunting. However, there are still some traditional pubs that either eschew food completely or else are of the opinion that chips and beer do not mix. I have given a general indication with each pub of the opening hours but during weekdays the publican is free to choose when to open, up to a maximum of twelve hours, and some change the hours to suit local demands. Sundays still have stricter restrictions and the normal hours are 12 noon to 3 pm and 7 pm to 10.30 pm – although remember that the Cat Inn at Enville, No 13, is unique in that its doors remain shut every Sunday! Nationwide though, Sunday hours are of course under government review. The hours when food is available are invariably shorter than the opening hours; but again, there is some variation as the 'open all day' pubs are more than happy to serve meals at any time.

The walker should find that the route descriptions and maps are sufficient to undertake the ramble without difficulty. However, it always adds interest if the relevant Ordnance Survey map in the

Landranger series is taken. Six are needed to cover the area of the walks in this book: number 127 Stafford and Telford, 128 Derby, 138 Kidderminster, 139 Birmingham, 140 Leicester and Coventry and 150 Worcester.

Remember that the countryside is constantly changing: stiles can be erected (or removed); waymarks can disappear; marker trees may be felled and hedges removed and so on. I have tried to describe the walk as accurately as possible.

Children are usually now welcomed into parts of most pubs but there are certain rules, so please check first; many have made provision with special menus, play areas and equipment to burn off surplus energy. I like to take my border collie Nell on walks; the law states that dogs are not allowed in those areas of pubs where food is served.

It only remains for me to wish you 'happy rambling' in Birmingham and Coventry's countryside and to assure you that you will enjoy some wonderful pubs at the same time.

Richard Shurey
Spring 1995

Area map showing locations of the walks.

① Great Haywood
The Fox and Hounds

Over the river Trent from Great Haywood is Cannock Chase, which was once a Royal forest and a great hunting ground. Mrs Sue Paul, licensee of this Ansells house for over ten years, tells me that deer hunted on the Chase used to be taken to the Fox and Hounds. The history of the present building can be traced back two centuries and it is appropriate that (besides the name of the pub) there are prints of hunting scenes on the walls of the lounge. The building is long and narrow and borders the road. Inside there are several different floor levels and two open fires in winter-time which give a cosy and homely atmosphere. The furnishings add to this, too, with plenty of benches and saddleback chairs.

The regular beers are Ansells and Tetley but there is a different guest beer each week, when I called it was Joules. There is a good selection for the lager and cider drinkers. There is a modest but reasonably priced menu and a specials board is alongside the bar. Vegetarians can select from several dishes, vegetable tagliatelle with mushroom and cream sauce is a popular choice. I also liked the idea of speciality evenings at the Fox and Hounds. The next one after my visit was to be given a Scandinavian theme. Children are welcomed at this pub and

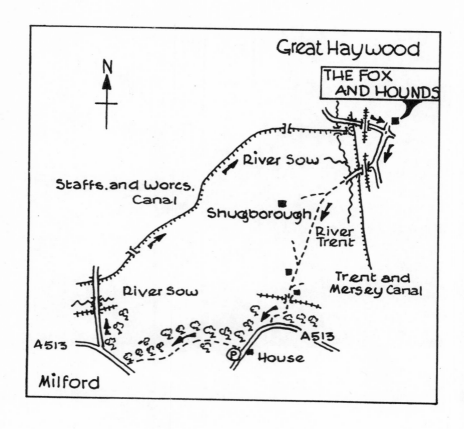

there is a small beer garden. Dogs can appreciate the warmth of the welcome if they are well-mannered.

The opening hours are from 12 noon to 11 pm Monday to Saturday; Sunday times are as usual.

Telephone: 01889 881252.

How to get there: Great Haywood is just off the A51, 4 miles north-west of Rugeley. The Fox and Hounds is on the left on entering the village.

Parking: There is a car park opposite the pub.

Length of the walk: 4½ miles. Map: OS Landranger series 127 Stafford and Telford and 128 Derby (inn GR 999230).

There are many interesting things to see on this short walk. Early on, the route goes over the 90-mile long Trent and Mersey Canal by using the Essex bridge. This former packhorse bridge of fourteen arches is the longest in England. Shugborough Hall was remodelled in the 1760s and has been the seat of the Anson family (the earls of Lichfield) since 1624. The return leg is beside the Staffordshire and Worcestershire Canal which was opened in 1772.

The Walk

Turn right from the car park and proceed to the centre of the village. As the road twists sharp left (by another inn) keep ahead. The narrow road goes under a railway then crosses the canal and river to enter the grounds of Shugborough.

Keep ahead, with the great house away over to the right. Follow the drive to the main road. Turn right; within ⅓ mile and opposite a house turn right into a track leading to the car park called Cold Man's Slade. Keep ahead along a broad track which skirts the wooded Satnall Hills then goes beside the walled border of Shugborough Park to the main road.

Turn right then soon right at a lane. The lane goes over the river Sow then to the canal bridge. Just before, go down steps left to the towpath. Turn right to go under the road and continue with the waterway on your left. After 1½ miles there is a meeting of canals.

Walk over the old canal by using the arched bridge then continue a few steps with the 'new' canal on the right then gain the road. Turn right to go over the waterway. The road leads to a junction at Great Haywood. The Fox and Hounds is to the left.

2 Little Haywood
The Red Lion

The Red Lion is a fine pub whose present building dates from 1935 but there has been a pub on this site for much longer. It was originally called the Bowyer's Arms after the family which was then at the mansion of Bishton Hall. The first known licensee in the 18th century was John Dean who fancied a change from his duties as footman at Hoar Cross Hall. The bar has simple but comfortable furnishings and the lounge is bright and light. There are old prints on the walls – I was especially interested in the one of the pub dated 1908.

One important difference distinguishes this from other pubs today – licensee Jim Louth dislikes the mixture of chips and beer in pubs so here speciality sandwiches are on offer. There is a wide choice of both hot and cold sandwiches, rolls and baps (which are served all day) with such fillings as tuna, turkey and steak. There is a choice of Marston's Pedigree Bitter, Banks's Mild or the periodically changing guest beer in the bar and lounge.

Squidge is the pub dog and he welcomes other well-behaved canine friends. Outside the pub looks a picture in summer-time when Tania Louth's garden prowess comes to the fore. She has won awards including Best Pub in the Staffordshire in Bloom contest. The pub is open 11 am to 11 pm Monday to Saturday and usual Sunday hours. Telephone: 01889 881314.

How to get there: Little Haywood is 3 miles north-west of Rugeley just off the A51. The pub is near the crossroads in the middle of the village.

Parking: There is a small car park at the side of the pub.

Length of the walk: 5 miles. Map: OS Landranger series 127 Stafford and Telford and 128 Derby (inn GR 004216).

The route goes through some delightful woodlands of Cannock Chase. The Chase has many herds of fallow deer — these are not often seen at close quarters but their footprints disclose their presence. Shugborough Park has several folly buildings and the route passes near the great house (the seat of the earls of Lichfield and now housing a county museum). The return leg is alongside the Trent and Mersey Canal. This was one of Brindley's masterpieces (although he died before its completion).

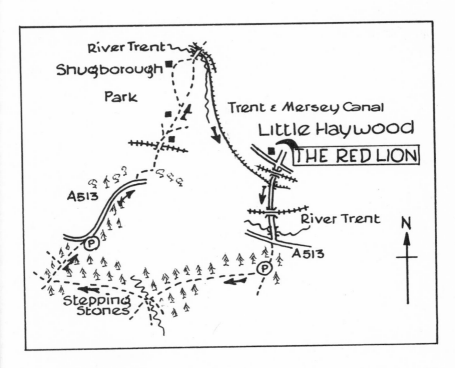

The Walk

Turn left out of the car park to the crossroads. Turn right. The narrow lane goes under two railways, and over the canal and river Trent. At the main road go straight over and along a vehicle track to a car park.

Continue to the far right-hand corner and go through a barrier. Walk along a wide track and then beside the fine woodlands of Cannock Chase. Come to the lovely place called 'Stepping Stones' where the water of a brook bubbles over the track. Beyond the water is a crossroads of tracks. Turn right now on the waymarked Staffordshire Way. Keep ahead then swing right at a junction of tracks.

Climb the rise then drop down to a picnic area and car park. Continue to the A513. Turn right. Within ½ mile turn left along a vehicle way to Shugborough. The vehicle way soon twists left and goes over a railway. In the parkland you can see the follies erected in the grounds by the Anson family. (There are also magnificent portals to the railway tunnels.)

Keep ahead at junctions with the tarmac drive. There is now a fine view of the great mansion of Shugborough. Go out of the parkland and cross the river Trent over 17th century Essex bridge – it once had forty arches but even with only fourteen remaining it is still the longest packhorse bridge in the land. Within a few steps you reach the canal; take the towpath right. Follow the waterway to the next road-bridge; gain the lane which was walked early on the outward leg. Retrace your steps to the crossroads and turn left to the Red Lion and those tasty sandwiches.

Acton Trussell
The Moat House

This pub reflects the history of Acton Trussell itself. Examination of the Moat House's timber frame during refurbishment points to a date of 1320 and it is then that the Trussells are first mentioned at Acton. Sir William Trussell of Kibblestone extended and refurbished the building as a hunting lodge for the vast Royal forest of Cannock Chase. The building is still complete with much of its moat, which was enlarged in the 18th century to form fishponds (to store fish before the age of refrigerators) while the west side was utilised by the canal builders. The Trussells were at Acton until 1658 when the house was acquired by the Anson family of Shugborough. It was only in 1988 that the splendid place was opened as the inn and restaurant called the Moat House. The owner has skilfully kept the feeling of the antiquity of the building whilst adding all the modern comforts of this age. Outside there are spacious lawns and willows dipping into the pools where swans glide lazily by. There are plenty of benches and tables to watch the tranquil scene while enjoying your refreshments after the walk.

The menu is not extensive but allied to the chef's specials of the day there is an excellent choice with vegetarians and children not

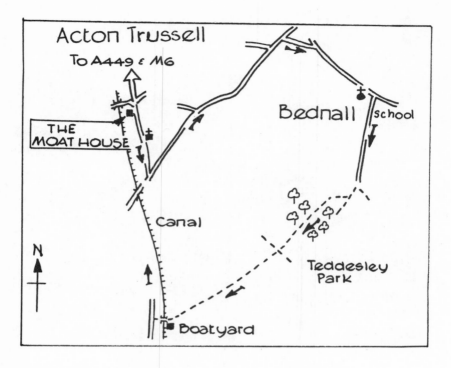

forgotten. The prices too are modest – the tasty home-made soup (always a good indication of a pub's pricing policy) was very good value when I called. The specials for the day included tiger prawns wrapped in filo pastry and a delicious pancake crammed with turkey and mushrooms.

The beers on offer are Banks's Bitter, Cameron's Red Ruby Bitter and Marston's Pedigree Bitter. Strongbow cider on draught is available and there is a good selection of lagers. The hours are 11 am to 3 pm, Monday to Friday, all day Saturday and normal Sunday hours. Telephone: 01785 712217.

How to get there: From Junction 13 on the M6 take the A449 Stafford road. Within ½ mile turn right to Acton Trussell. The pub is at the far end of the village on the right.

Parking: At the side of the pub.

Length of the walk: 5 miles. Map: OS Landranger series 127 Stafford and Telford (inn GR 936177).

14

The walk is through a mainly pastoral countryside and the parkland of Teddesley Park. The return leg is alongside the towpath of the Staffordshire and Worcestershire Canal which was engineered by James Brindley and opened in 1772.

The Walk

Out of the car park turn right along the lane. Pass the little village church which is over 600 years old with a 16th century tower. At a T-junction turn left. Within 1 mile take a lane right which is signed to Bednall. Just past the church (rebuilt last century) turn right down a lane signed No Through Road. Pass the little school and take a right fork when the way divides.

Within 100 yards a path is signed right. Walk alongside a left-hand hedge. At the end of the hedge climb a stile to a pasture on the left. Follow the arrowed direction over the field towards a wood. Go into the wood and out the other side and cross a brook.

The heading is now constant with stiles to show the way. The path is well walked along the Staffordshire Way which crosses a farm road. Through parkland cross another bridge. Heading towards the buildings of a boatyard cross a field to a rather concealed stile by a wooden gate. Cross the canal and gain the towpath. Walk with water on your right. At bridge 92 (Acton Moat bridge) leave the waterway. Go over the canal to an estate road. The pub is on your right.

Cannock Wood
The Park Gate Inn

4

This pub is just a stone's throw (or perhaps a javelin throw) from the earthworks of one of the finest hill-forts in the land. Castle Ring was built on one of the highest points (800 ft) in Staffordshire in about 500 BC. The pub is much more recent – from about 1640 – and was once part of the estate of the Marquis of Anglesey. A local told me that the pub was once known as the Anchor. I am a little sceptical about the reason – that from the top of Castle Ring, ships at anchor could be seen off Liverpool.

The place was said to have been the scene of many a banquet and what is now the refurbished Timbers Restaurant was used by agents to collect the dues for the master. A special feature in the single large lounge are the two snug alcoves each side of the inglenook fireplace – just right for that cosy tête-a-tête. There is plenty of polished brass, too.

The choice of food is daunting but I was impressed by the fish dishes, especially the Big Catch platter and the grilled fresh whiting. Vegetarians have a selection from which to choose and half portions (but with plenty of chips) are available for children. Sorry Fido but you will have to stay outside with Nell. The beers on offer are Holt's Mild,

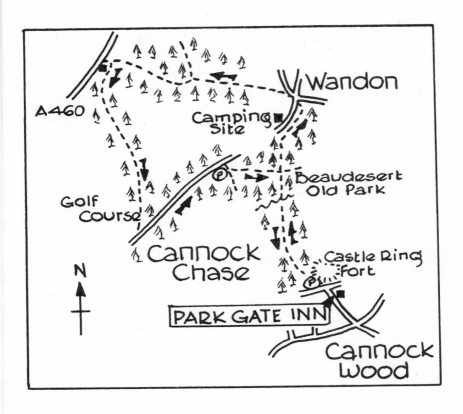

Burton Bitter and Marston's Pedigree. For cider drinkers there is Gaymer's Olde English.

Outside is a well-equipped play area including a bouncy castle and there are plenty of benches and tables from which to admire the view far over the valley. The opening hours are from 11 am to 11 pm Monday to Saturday and the usual limited hours on Sundays.

Telephone: 01543 682223.

How to get there: All the surrounding roads are well signed to nearby Castle Ring.

Parking: Park at the side and front of the pub.

Length of the walk: 5 miles. Map: OS Landranger series 128 Derby (inn GR 046125).

The walk is over lands of Cannock Chase which formerly all belonged to the Marquis of Anglesey. These were from Norman times great hunting grounds, and even today herds of fallow deer roam the uplands and are a hazard to drivers on the roads. Much of the land is planted with pines and administered by the Forestry Commission. The Chase was designated an Area of Outstanding Natural Beauty in 1958.

The Walk

Turn right out of the car park and walk along the road to a T-junction. Go straight over to a car park at the hill-fort. Keep ahead along a wide track alongside left-hand woods and with the earthworks now on your right side.

Maintain the direction at junctions with other pathways and soon drop steeply downhill. Go over a brook and pass some pools. The track now climbs out of the valley. Go straight over at a crossroads of tracks. Immediately before a road the path is signed to the right.

The path runs alongside the left-hand road then joins the road. Turn right to a junction. Turn left then at once take a rough vehicle track on the left. This is also signed as the Heart of England Way. When the track divides the Way takes the right-hand fork. We take the left fork and continue ahead. Just before a barrier and a road go along a track through a barrier left.

Veer around to the right to a junction of tracks near a house. Go over the hill and continue past a golf course and proceed to a road. Turn left. Within ⅓ mile turn right into the car park of Beaudesert Old Park. At once take the wide track through a barrier left. The track leads to a crossroads of tracks. Turn right and retrace your steps to the Castle Ring and the pub.

5 Brewood
The Three Stirrups

This is a pub with a rather obscure pedigree; Brewood is a medieval market town where time stood still while Wolverhampton, down the road, flourished. The Three Stirrups may once have been a coaching inn on the edge of the community. Keith Taylor (assisted by Lynne Jones who looks after the kitchen) has been at this Banks's pub for some half a dozen years. Lynne is also responsible for the magnificent floral displays that adorn the walls and gardens.

There is a cosy old-fashioned bar and a large separate modernised dining room/lounge. This is a pub where darts and dominoes are popular. There is a set menu and the specials of the day are displayed in the lounge. There was a surf and turf dish which was new to me – it turned out to be a combination of steak and scampi. Vegetarians will always find something to their taste: when I called the vegetable moussaka was proving popular.

There are Banks's and Marston's beers and a choice of draught Scrumpy Jack and Strongbow ciders. Both children and dogs (in the bar only) are welcome. Children's meals are available and there is a play area to burn off that surplus energy after the walk. There are benches in the garden.

The opening hours are usually 11 am to 11 pm Monday to Saturday

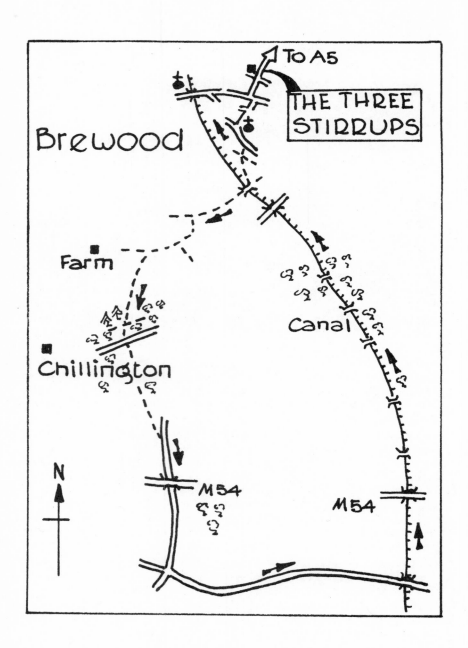

To A5

THE THREE
STIRRUPS

Brewood

Farm

Canal

Chillington

M54

M54

N

and 12 noon to 3 pm and 7 pm to 10.30 pm on Sunday.
Telephone: 01902 850243.

How to get there: From the centre of Brewood take the Gailey and
Penkridge road opposite the oriental-looking Speedwell Castle. The
pub is at a crossroads on the left.

Parking: There is car park beside the pub.

Length of the walk: 6 miles. Map: OS Landranger series 127 Stafford and
Telford (inn GR 884090).

*The walk starts at Brewood – the town has some magnificent buildings to visit
before or after the walk. There is Brewood Convent which was once the workhouse.
Nearby is the splendid Speedwell Castle (the building was paid for out of the winnings
on a racehorse called Speedwell). The parish church has a prominent spire which tops
168 ft.*

The Walk
Come out of the car park into Shop Lane. Turn left then at once right
at the crossroads to the centre of Brewood. Cross to the road
opposite. Church Road leads to the church dedicated to St Mary and
St Chad. The main road sweeps left; keep along this for a few steps
then right along a footpath through a brick arch. The unsigned path
leads to a rough vehicle way. Go almost opposite and follow the
footpath over pastures to a canal bridge. Turn right along the wide
track to cross the waterway. You are now walking along Hyde Mill
Lane. When the track divides take the left way to keep straight ahead
to pass a farm on the right.
    Look for a stile on the left. Walk at the side of a field to a corner
stile. Follow Staffordshire Way signs with stiles to show the way. Veer
right to the avenue of Chillington Hall by a plantation of Norwegian
pines. There are some fine oaks in the avenue. (The Hall – the seat
of the Giffard family – is to the right.)
    Cross the drive along an arrowed way to a road. Pass through a
kissing-gate and keep at the left-hand edge of a pasture along a well
worn track. Maintain the heading to a corner stile. Cross a green way
and keep the direction past a pool to a road. This is Port Way. Turn
right to cross a motorway. A crossroads is reached.
    Turn left and follow a lane to a canal bridge. Immediately after go
through a white gate on the right. Go under the road and along the
towpath (water now on left side). Just before a bridge (numbered 14)
climb steps to the road. Turn right along High Green then ahead to the
town centre. Retrace your steps left to the pub.

6 Wall
The Trooper

One would expect the soldier on the sign would be a Roman legionary as the ruins of the Roman fort are only a good spear throw away, but the trooper depicted is from many centuries later! However, this is a house which would satisfy any soldier's appetite for the Super Trooper steaks are renowned – there are six types on offer in this Ansells pub. There are also specials of the day which are listed on a board over the bar. I found the cod in a prawn sauce and cheese chicken and the minted Barnsley chops good value. Children are welcome inside if they are eating – they have their own menu on which chips feature prominently.

There are two bars and a restaurant; the simple Roman Bar has a tiled floor and is ideal for walking boots while the Trooper Lounge is very homely to enjoy that special meal. We are politely informed that 'meals are not instant – they are prepared especially with only you in mind'. Beers available are Burton Ale, Caffreys Irish Ale, and Ansells Bitter and Mild.

There is a large garden with plenty of benches. Pub opening hours are 11 am to 3 pm and 6 pm to 11 pm Monday to Saturday and 12 noon to 3 pm and 6 pm to 10.30 pm on Sundays.

Telephone: 01543 480413.

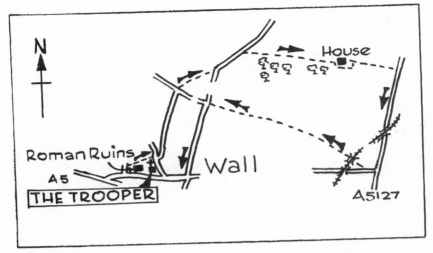

How to get there: Wall is situated off the A5127 about 1½ miles north of Shenstone. Follow the signs to the Roman ruins at Wall. The pub is at a road junction to the east of the village.

Parking: There is a car park at the rear of the pub.

Length of the walk: 3 miles. Map: OS Landranger series 139 Birmingham (inn GR 100065).

Wall is now a tiny village but to the Romans it was called Letocetum and of great importance being at the junction of Watling Street and Ryknield Street. The excavated ruins are of great interest and there is a small museum of finds.

The Walk

From the car park turn right then right again to keep the inn on the right. Go past the entrance to the interesting site of the Roman fort which was called Letocetum. Turn right by a telephone box. Within a few steps turn right along a vehicle track and you now overlook the Roman ruins.

The vehicle track becomes a green way and leads to a lane by Wall church. Turn right then at once left along a narrow lane signed to Lichfield. The lane is squeezed between banks to a T-junction. Go through the opposite gate and walk to the far right-hand corner of the field.

Go through a corner gap to a lane. Turn left. Within 300 yards take an unsigned path over a stile on the right. Walk along a tractor way to pass to the left of a round wood.

We are now at some height and have a splendid view of the three spires of Lichfield Cathedral – the 'Three Ladies of the Vale'. Still to the left of the wood walk over the open field (often sown) to pass through a gate (the left of two adjoining gates).

Keep a new wood on the right to again walk over an open field and now walk alongside a left-hand wood to a corner stile near a white house. Continue through a pasture, keeping the garden and house on the left side.

Join the vehicle drive and walk along this to the A5127. Turn right along the pavement beside the main road. Take the next lane on the right. Within 100 yards take a wide track through a metal gate on the right. Pass under the railway and keep on the vehicle track to a lane. Turn left then right to return to the Trooper.

7 Little Hay
The Hollybush

Visit this well-run pub in the quiet village of Little Hay on a summer's day and immediately you will be overwhelmed by the magnificent floral display. Step over the threshold and this same indication of pride in the pub is obvious. The pub's history is a little obscure but it was a rural hostelry at the turn of the century. After the recent refurbishment there is an open lounge and restaurant area but also soft lighting, plenty of dark oak and many cosy corners for discussing the walk.

Ruth Perks oversees the cooking and has won many awards for her culinary efforts. On the day I called there was fresh salmon and the beef in Stilton looked tempting. There is a full children's menu and often a promotion when youngsters dine free with their parents.

Keith Perks holds the certificate of the Guild of Master Cellarmen so there is a good range of well-kept beers. The choice is between Ind Coope Burton Ale, Tetley's Cask Conditioned Bitter, Ansells Bitter and Mild. There are several lagers and ciders available (including an excellent draught Olde English).

The house golden retrievers (Kim and Bonnie) are not allowed in the pub so canine visitors must stay outside where there is a pretty beer garden and a play area for children. The opening hours are 11.30 am to 3 pm and 6 pm to 11 pm Monday to Saturday and 12 noon to 3 pm and 7 pm to 10.30 pm on Sunday.

Telephone: 01543 481217.

How to get there: About 2 miles south of Shenstone along the A5127 take a lane left. Bear left at a junction. The Hollybush is a further 1 mile on the right.

Parking: There is a car park at the side and rear of the pub.

Length of the walk: 3½ miles. Map: OS Landranger series 139 Birmingham (inn GR 122029).

The walk is over gentle countryside where there are few hills. It is mixed farmland and the paths are not always well defined but route finding should not prove difficult.

The Walk

Directly opposite the car park a footpath is signed. Walk alongside a right-hand hedge through several fields which are often sown and keep a constant heading to the A5127. Turn right for about 300 yards.

Turn left through the gateway of Croft Farm. The path is signed. Walk between barns and along a tractor way under a railway.

Keep the heading over an arable field, aiming just to the left of a white house. Climb a stile to a lane. Turn left. There is now some fine

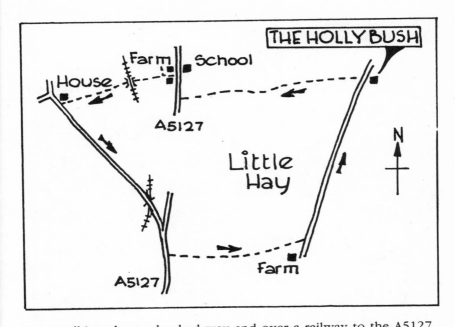

lane walking along a banked way and over a railway to the A5127.

Turn right. Within a few hundred yards a path is signed on the left. Walk at the side of a left then right-hand hedge following the line of overhead power cables; climb a rise to a step stile to a pasture. Still on the same heading walk by a left-hand field boundary (with a farm away to the right).

Drop down to a corner stile by a gateway. Continue over a meadow (left-hand hedge) to a step stile to a lane. The Hollybush is about 1 mile to the left along the lane.

Codsall
The Wheel Inn

This pub was once a small cottage built sometime in the last century on the Wolverhampton road. Since those days it has been greatly added to and skilfully modernised to provide a pleasant pub on the edge of a large village. The heavy old beams are still visible inside and there is a bright but homely appearance about the bars.

All the food is home-made. It is good plain cooking such as cottage pie or steak and kidney pie but there are always specials chalked on a board near the bar. For the hungry rambler there is a good selection of sandwiches and 'Kids' Meals' are also available. Flintstones (chicken) and Dinosaurs (fish) with the inevitable chips and peas are always popular. The beers served are the full range of Banks's (Bitter, Mild and Pedigree) and the lagers include the rather rarer Czech draught Zamek. For the cider drinkers the choice is between bottled Strongbow or draught Woodpecker.

There is a recreation ground adjacent for outdoor dining and this is fine for Fido too as dogs are not allowed in the pub. Saturday is all day opening; Monday to Friday hours are 11.30 am to 4 pm and 7 pm to 11 pm with normal Sunday hours.

Telephone: 01902 842189.

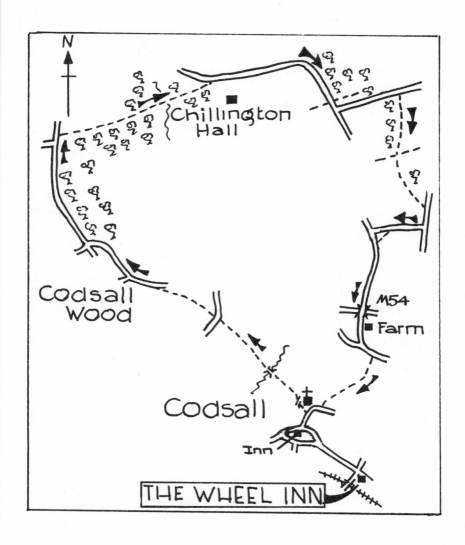

How to get there: From the centre of Codsall take the Wolverhampton road. The Wheel Inn is a few hundred yards along on the right.

Parking: There is car park at the side and rear of the pub.

Length of the walk: 6 miles. Map: OS Landranger series 127 Stafford and Telford (inn GR 867035).

The walk is around the park of Chillington Hall. There was a medieval house on the site followed by a Tudor residence. In the 18th century the present magnificent mansion was built for the Giffard family and Capability Brown went to work on the garden.

The Walk

From the car park turn left along the Wolverhampton road towards the centre of Codsall. Stay on the main road then turn right along Church Road. The church (rebuilt in 1848 but with a tower 600 years old) is at the top of the rise. Go left through the churchyard and out through the gate at the far side. Cross to the opposite path.

The path descends alongside a cemetery towards the valley. Keep ahead through a kissing-gate and alongside a hedge. Cross a brook and maintain the direction to walk the way of tractors to a vehicle drive leading to a lane. Take the signed path opposite and follow the arrowed direction over a field. The paths are now through meadows with stiles to show the way. Keep to the right of a new house. Over a stile walk alongside a left-hand hedge to a new stile to a lane. Turn left and keep ahead at a junction. At the next meeting of roads turn right (signed Boscobel). The road goes over a motorway; ½ mile beyond turn right down a farm vehicle way which is signed as a bridleway.

Keep on a constant direction along the border of a large wood then through the trees. The track emerges on a lane and turn right. Away to the right is Chillington Hall. The lane crosses the drive to the big house then at once take the lane left which runs parallel to the drive. Within ½ mile turn right through a kissing-gate.

Walk along the left-hand edge of the pasture along a well worn path. Maintain the heading to a corner stile. Cross a green way and keep the direction past a pool and follow the waymarked Staffordshire Way to a road. Turn right; within 200 yards take a road signed Chillington on the right. Drop downhill then after ¼ mile climb a stile on the left by a gate. Continue along a tarmac way (Gunstone Lane) and cross a motorway. Keep along this way to a junction of lanes. Turn left. Within 200 yards climb a stile on the right. In a meadow walk alongside the fence. Keep ahead through fields to a farm and vehicle way to Codsall and the pub.

⑨ Middleton
The Green Man

The Green Man is on a no through road on the edge of the quiet village. It is a building full of character and was probably originally a farmhouse. The farmer would hang a green flag outside when the beer was ready – hence the name. The place has been a public house from around 1920.

Like all good 16th century buildings, ghosts lurk in the Green Man. An old lady and 'Harry' are the favourite spectral figures. Open fires give a warm welcome in winter-time in the pleasant oak-beamed horseshoe-shaped lounge where a large range of meals is served. The quality of the steaks is well known and there is a daily delivery of fresh fish. There are plenty of favourite meals 'with chips' for children. Vegetarians are also catered for.

The beers are M and B Brew XI and Mild and Worthington. There is a good choice of lagers and ciders and how cheering to see a good reasonably-priced house wine available.

The hours of opening are 11 am to 3 pm and 5.30 pm to 11 pm Monday to Saturday and 12 noon to 3 pm and 7 pm to 10.30 pm Sunday. It is pleasant in summer to sit underneath the huge sun umbrellas in the garden and solve the world's problems.

Telephone: 0121 308 6688.

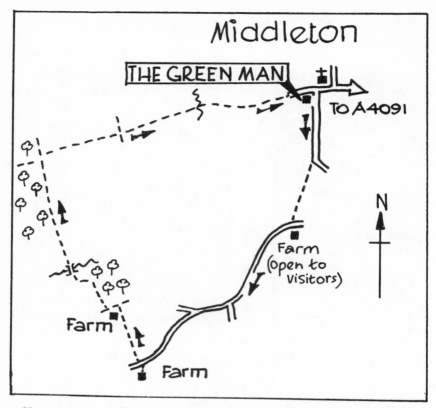

How to get there: 4 miles south of Tamworth turn right along a lane signed to Middleton. The inn is at the far end of the village on the left.

Parking: There is a car park at the side of the pub.

Length of the walk: 3½ miles. Map: OS Landranger series 139 Birmingham (inn GR 176983).

Middleton is a quiet rural backwater between main roads. The clock has stopped at about 12 for many years and this just about sums up the unchanging countryside of the route. The return is through woodlands where bluebells are a delight in spring.

The Walk

From the car park turn right; at once turn right again along a leafy lane. Within 400 yards an unsigned path starts on the right. As the lane bends left go through a gap to an arable field on the right. Take a direction to an electricity pylon then continue to a far corner gap. On the lane turn right. (To the left is an open farm which delights children.)

The lane twists this way and that. Go past two junctions. After about a mile and opposite a farm drive climb a stile on the right. Take the arrowed direction in the pasture to go over a ditch and fence stile.

Walk by a right-hand hedge to a metal gate to a farm drive. Turn left and follow the arrowed way to the right of the farm. Climb a stile by a metal gate and drop downhill along a tractor way. At a junction of tracks stay on the tractor way which swings left. Follow this to a bridge over a brook.

Across the water walk over an open field to the right-hand corner of a wood. Follow the path at the right-hand edge of the woodlands. After about 400 yards turn right along a path which hugs a field boundary. The well used track leads to a farm vehicle way which goes to Middleton and the Green Man.

10 Trysull
The Bell Inn

As the pub records, the Bell Inn, with a building dating from the 18th century, has seen many changes over the years but remains a social and convivial centre of a small community. The first recorded landlord was Benjamin Richards in 1829. Like many inns in those days the landlord was also the brewer and specialised in a mild ale which was heavy, dark, sweet and strong (at a gravity of 1060, the second highest in England) and varied from brew to brew. The place was allowed to remain open as long as there was an empty bed for travellers.

The present licensee came to the Bell in 1994 and the pub now advertises that it 'offers something for everyone'. There is a fine homely atmosphere in the restaurant, lounge and bars; children (and dogs in the Countryman Bar) are welcomed and half portions of the fare are offered. There is a full à la carte menu in the restaurant and tasty and home-made dishes from the bar.

Particularly popular is the lasagne and steak chasseur with special sauces. Vegetarians always have a choice of four dishes. The full range of Holden's beers are on offer; in addition there are guest beers – when I called they were from Beamish and Bathams. The cider drinkers can have Scrumpy Jack or Autumn Gold and the lager choice is between Kronenbourg or Carling Black Label.

Outside there is a neat appearance to this house with plenty of hanging baskets and flowers in summer-time. There are benches and tables on the terraces for those warmer days. I was particularly intrigued by the old pump which constantly fills up the horse's water trough. The hours are 11.30 am to 2.30 pm and 5.30 pm to 11 pm Monday to Saturday and the usual times on Sundays.

Telephone: 01902 892871.

How to get there: Halfway between Wolverhampton and Kingswinford on the A449 there is a roundabout at the junction with the A463. Take the road westwards and follow signs to Trysull. The Bell is in the centre of the village next to the church.

Parking: There is a car park at the side and rear of the pub.

Length of the walk: 9 miles. Map: OS Landranger series 139 Birmingham and 138 Kidderminster (inn GR 853943).

Trysull, a village which was on the periphery of Kinver Forest, was recorded in the Domesday Survey of 1086. It was originally known as Tresel — a Celtic name for the Smestow Brook. The walk follows the Staffordshire Way along the escarpment of Abbot's Castle Hill; this two-mile upland is composed of Bunter Pebble Beds and rises to over 400 ft. At the northern end are the earthworks from the occupation by the Romans.

The Walk

Out of the car park turn left to a crossroads. Keep ahead and follow the lane to the hamlet of Seisdon. Opposite is a signed footpath. Follow the clear way which goes through a garden and over an estate road. Maintain the heading through fields to a lane.

Turn left to a T-junction. Continue left for a few steps then right down a farm vehicle way. Follow Staffordshire Way signs. At a T-junction of farm tracks our way is left to a lane with the lovely name of Tinker's Castle Road. Turn right for 400 yards. At the top of the rise and near a rather unusual castle-like house take a path left.

Climb the slope and continue along a fenced way. You are now walking along Abbot's Castle Hill. The track maintains a constant heading to emerge through barriers on the B4176. Cross almost opposite to a signed path down a farm tractor way. At the bottom of the slope and under power lines our path goes 90 degrees left.

The path is at the edges of fields then passes sand pits. Keep the buildings on your right and walk along the drive to a road. Turn left then at once right along New Road. Stay on this lane to a junction at

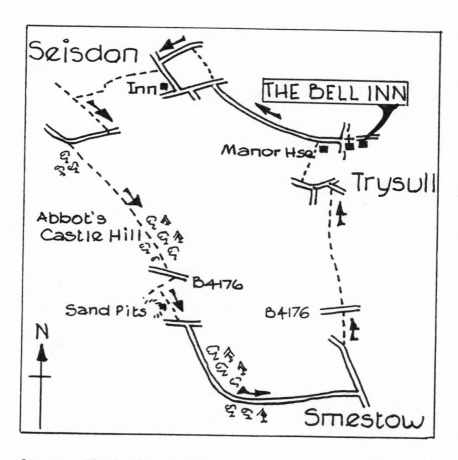

Smestow. The hamlet gives its name to a brook which means the unflattering 'stagnant pool'.

Turn left at the T-junction and climb the rise. As the road bends sharp left on the brow of the hill climb a stile ahead. The waymark arrow shows the direction to take at the side of pastures to a stile to the B4176. Cross to the vehicle way opposite which is signed as a bridleway.

Keep a fairly constant heading past buildings to a lane. Turn left. Turn left again at a road junction. Keep ahead at another junction. Within 200 yards take a signed bridleway along a wide track on the right to emerge on a road near the Manor House. The Bell Inn is a few hundred yards to the right.

36

11 Kingsbury
The Royal Oak

As pubs go, this fine village pub is quite new, having only been a public house from about 1920. Before that the village blacksmith and wheelwright was here. Managers Dennis and Shirley Eastwood have built up a reputation for good food and drink. The flowers, tubs and hanging baskets are a delight in summer and inside all is gleaming brasses and cosiness. Also gleaming are the sports trophies, for the Royal Oak runs football and darts teams.

There is always a good choice of beers with Marston's Pedigree, Banks's Mild, John Smith's Bitter and a guest ale which changes every two weeks. The choice of the standard food is augmented with specials which are chalked on a board by the bar. The chicken tangy lemon and Royal Oak grill looked most appetizing. Major, the house great Dane, requests that canine visitors remain outside.

The opening hours are 12 noon to 2.30 pm and 6 pm to 11 pm Monday to Saturday and 12 noon to 3 pm and 6 pm to 10.30 pm on Sunday with 'food hours' rather less. Families are welcomed with special low prices for children's drinks and snacks.

Telephone: 01827 872339.

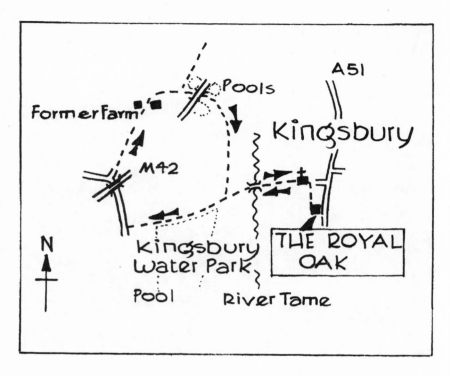

How to get there: Kingsbury is on the A51 four miles south of Tamworth. The pub is at the far end of the village on the right.

Parking: There is a car park beside the pub.

Length of the walk: 2½ miles. Map: OS Landranger series 139 Birmingham (inn GR 216963).

Kingsbury is an ancient and historic village for here was a 'bury' or fortified house for the King of Mercia. The church near the pub is 12th century and there is also a school founded in 1686. The walk is through the Water Park and returns over the river Tame.

The Walk

From the far corner of the car park go through the railings and (with the church away to the left) maintain the heading over a recreation ground to a hard path. Turn left alongside the churchyard. The ruins of the old fortified Manor House are on the right.

Go down steps and along the path to the bridge over the river

Tame. Still keep the heading over river pastures and through the Kingsbury Water Park which has been created from old gravel workings. This is a most interesting route with a vast sheet of water on the left and wildfowl gathering everywhere.

Maintain the direction along hard tracks to pass an information centre and car park. Follow the vehicle way to a lane. Turn right over a motorway. Within 300 yards the lane twists sharp left. Take a vehicle way on the right.

Past former farm buildings take a track on the right which goes by little meres and under a motorway again. Keep ahead at junctions to join the outward path. Turn left to recross the river and retrace your steps to the pub.

12 Hartshill Green
The Stag and Pheasant

The Stag and Pheasant is a simple rural hostelry offering good but basic fare before or after the walk which begins in nearby Hartshill Country Park. The locals still talk of the time when most of the customers were miners or quarry workers; however, all the local pits have now closed. As in those past days, this is still a community pub; it is the base for football teams, darts, pool, and dominoes are played and there are quiz nights. Perhaps some of the literary questions are on the poet Michael Draycott who was born in a cottage opposite the pub in 1563.

The full range of Flowers beers are offered and there is Red Rock and Dry Blackthorn on draught for those whose taste is more to cider. Bar snacks are available but this is more a drinker's pub and not so suitable for children. Fine for dogs though! Outside are benches and tables on a terrace.

The Stag and Pheasant is conveniently open all day Saturday. Apart from Sunday, which has the normal opening hours, the hours for the rest of the week are 12 noon to 2.30 pm and 5.30 pm to 11 pm.

Telephone: 01203 393173.

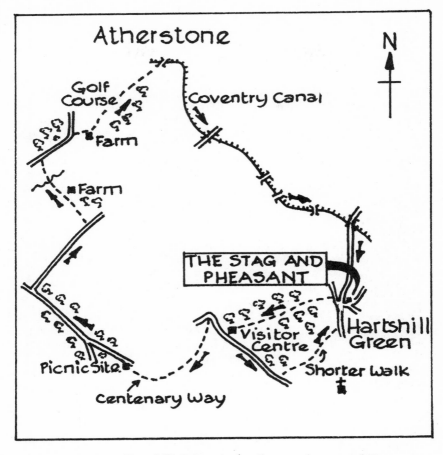

Atherstone

How to get there: Hartshill Green is 4 miles north-west of Nuneaton. Take the B4114 and B4111. Take the first left after the canal bridge to Hartshill Green. The pub is on the Green.

Parking: There are quiet roads around the Green.

Length of the walk: 8 miles or 2 miles (shortened route). Map: OS Landranger series 140 Leicester and Coventry (inn GR 946325).

The route starts through Hartshill Country Park. Covering 135 acres, much of the area is wooded with both deciduous and coniferous trees. The next stage follows part of the Centenary Way — the long distance waymarked route through Warwickshire. The return leg is along the towpath of the Coventry Canal which was planned by James Brindley and completed in 1790.

41

The Walk

Cross the Green (going to the right of the shelter which commemorates the birthplace of Michael Draycott) and the main road to the new flats. At the right of the flats take a signed path. Within a few steps two paths are signed. Take the left-hand one.

Go through a barrier and down the steps to cross a brook. Enter the woods. Keeping ahead climb the slope and maintain the heading over crossing paths. Still keep ahead at a marker post (numbered 4) to drop down to a railed footbridge over a brook.

Climb to a T-junction of tracks by the post numbered 3. Turn left then at once right to resume climbing. The path twists around to a car park (Visitor Centre). *For the shorter walk* turn left on the lane; just before the houses on the left take a footpath through a gate; walk by the right-hand edge of the woods to climb steps to the road. The pub is to the left.

For the long walk turn right on the lane. Within ⅓ mile take a signed path over a stile left. This is marked as the Centenary Way. Cross the fields to reach the route of an old railway. Walk to the right along the cutting lined with bushes. Climb stiles (still following Centenary Way waymarks) to a picnic area and a road.

Turn left to a T-junction. Turn right. Within ½ mile turn right along Purley Chase Lane. After ½ mile turn left; the footpath is signed down a vehicle drive. Keep ahead past a farm to drop down the valley. Cross a brook to a golf course. Climb to the top right-hand corner to a lane. Turn right.

After ⅓ mile turn right down the drive of Outwoods Farm. Beyond the farm enter a golf course. Walk near the right-hand border to a bridge over a canal. Gain the towpath. Walk alongside the waterway for about 2 miles to a roadbridge by a waterways depot.

Gain the road and climb the hill to Hartshill Green and the pub.

13 Enville
The Cat Inn

I was told by John Johnson (who runs this freehouse with Lisa Bowen) that the name of the pub is an answer to a Trivial Pursuit question 'Which pub is closed on Sundays?'. The building is part of the Enville Estate and by tradition has always had the 'Closed' sign on Sundays. One guide book suggests that the restriction was imposed because customers of the inn – which opens directly onto the street – blocked the road with their horses.

The Cat Inn has provided country fare to locals and travellers since the 16th century. The restaurant was once a granary and the bars comprise several adjoining small rooms where open fires are a feature in winter-time. There are heavy beamed ceilings adorned with horse brasses, settles and benches. Prints of scenes of old cricket XIs and country vistas hang on the walls.

There are three menus (plus the specials board) covering the bars and restaurant but the dishes available emphasise that this is rural England so we find game and pheasant pie, poacher's platter (rabbit and venison) and so on. Vegetarians are not forgotten with such delicacies as peasant's pot (a blend of beans and pulses). No special provision is made for children.

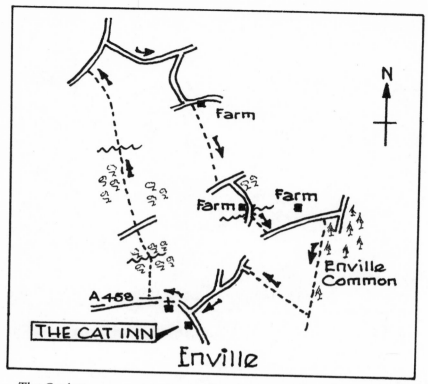

Enville

The Cat has a reputation for its beer. There is a local Enville brewery which for three years has supplied bitter and its strong Gothic Beer (at a strength of 1052). In addition there are Theakston XB and two guest ales which are changed weekly. All the beers (and their strengths) are chalked on a notice by the dart board. McEwan's lager is available and cider drinkers can choose between Scrumpy Jack and Strongbow.

The weekday and Saturday opening hours are from 12 noon to 2.30 pm and 7 pm to 11 pm.

Excepting Sundays, for the rest of the week the Cat Inn is a splendid hostelry providing good food and drink plus bed and breakfast accommodation and a self-contained apartment.

Telephone: 01384 872209.

How to get there: Enville is 5 miles out of Stourbridge along the A458 Bridgnorth road. The Cat Inn is in the centre of the village on the left.

Parking: You may park at the side of the pub (car park not available on Sundays).

Length of the walk: 5 miles. Map: OS Landranger series 138 Kidderminster (inn GR 826868).

Part of the route is along the Staffordshire Way — a long distance path which takes a circuitous route through the county from Mow Cop in the north then southwards to Kinver Edge. Early on the walk Enville's church is passed. Although on a Norman foundation, the restoration by Sir Gilbert Scott in the last century included the marvellous tower which followed the style of Gloucester Cathedral.

The Walk

Out of the car park turn left to go by the church. Within 400 yards turn right by a house drive. The path is signed at the border of the grass to a white metal gate in the corner. Keep ahead to climb step stiles then walk through a wood. Continue ahead to cross a brook and then along a path to a lane.

Go directly across to a signed path. Walk at the side of a field then maintain the direction along a waymarked path beside a wood. Follow the path over a stream and continue to a lane. Turn right then right again at a junction. Within ½ mile is a junction of lanes.

Take the right-hand way. The lane twists this way then that. Just after a sharp bend to the left and before a farm take a bridleway on the right. The bridleway leads to a lane. Turn left then at once right at a junction.

Within 400 yards go past Morfe Hall Farm and over a brook. Immediately take the bridleway left to a lane. Turn left. After ½ mile and before a junction of lanes take a wide cart track on the right. The track borders left-hand woodlands. When you reach a meeting of ways turn right along a farm vehicle track.

Follow the clear way to Browns Lake Road then Blundies Lane. Turn left. This leads to the A458 and almost opposite is the Cat Inn.

14 Whittington
The Whittington Inn

This fine pub is a listed building with an interesting history. The Whittingtons (yes, related to the famous Dick!) were first noted in the records of 1307 when Sir William was the owner of all Kinver. He erected the present building in 1310. This is yet another house where Charles II stayed a night after his flight from the Battle of Worcester! From here he fled to White Ladies and Boscobel. In 1711 Queen Anne visited.

The Manor House did not become an inn until 1783 when the licence was transferred from the old Whittington Inn which was then in another building. You can still see parts of the walled Tudor garden and the moat but the real splendours of the pub are inside. There are five bars; many are oak panelled and everywhere are quaint corners, huge beams and uprights and low doorways.

The food is home-made and superb. Specials of the day are available to augment the regular menu – there was roast turkey and stuffing when I called in September! Vegetarians are always well catered for and Sunday lunches are served. There is a wide range of beers – the real ale is Camerons Strongarm. In addition you can sample the full range of Wolverhampton & Dudley Breweries' ales and Marston's

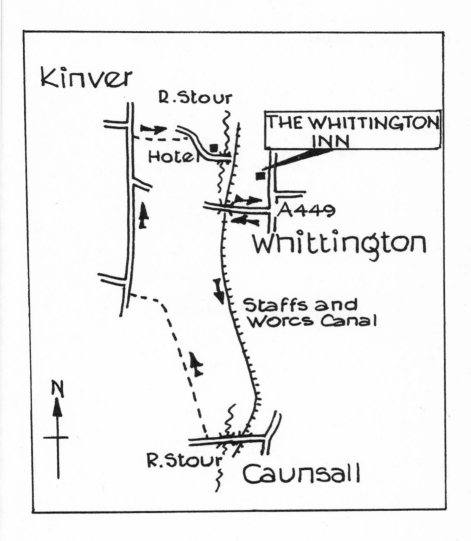

Pedigree. Families are welcome and children always have a good choice, with pizzas popular. My collie Nell was happy to abide by the rules and stay outside to admire the view.

The pub is open from 11 am to 3 pm and 5.30 pm to 11 pm Monday to Saturday and 12 noon to 3 pm and 7 pm to 10.30 pm on Sunday.

Telephone: 01384 872110.

How to get there: The pub is on the left on the A449, 4 miles north of Kidderminster.

Parking: There is a car park at the side of the pub.

Length of the walk: 3 miles. Map: OS Landranger series 138 Kidderminster and 139 Birmingham (inn GR 856828).

Part of the walk follows the towpath of the Staffordshire and Worcestershire Canal which hugs the valley of the river Stour and is one of the contour canals of the old pattern. It was engineered by James Brindley and opened to traffic in 1772. It became one of the more lucrative waterways paying high dividends to the lucky shareholders.

The Walk

Leave the car park and turn right along the A449. Within 300 yards turn right down a lane called Windsor Holloway. The narrow way drops down to the canal. Turn left along the towpath with the water on your left side.

Leave the canal at the next roadbridge at the village of Caunsall. Walk along the lane and cross the river Stour. After a few yards a path is signed on the right over a stile (also signed as the long distance way, the North Worcestershire Path).

Follow the waymarked path to a road. Turn right. Go past a road junction. Four hundred yards further climb a bank right on a signed path. Follow the indicated direction to cross a meadow to a kissing-gate to a lane. Turn right to drop down to a hotel.

Walk along the vehicle way to go over the river Stour. A few steps further is the canal again. Turn right and follow the waterway to the first lane, Windsor Holloway. Retrace your steps to the Whittington Inn.

15 Clent
The Fountain Inn

This place has been supplying good ale and food for many centuries; it was once called the Rock Fountain when a gush of water from the Clent Hills tumbled from a spring at the front of the building. Today it looks very welcoming with hanging baskets in summer-time and a warm atmosphere in winter. There are inglenooks and cosy corners, also many interesting knick-knacks including old guns and weapons and prints of old England. The pub has a skittle alley.

Besides the standard menu of food there are always daily specials like fresh chicken breast filled with pâté in a Madeira sauce, chalked on a board by the bar; the vegetarians have a dish of their own, such as mushroom, nut and pasta bake. There is a children's menu with the favourite fish tiddlers. This is a Wolverhampton and Dudley Breweries' house and it sells a full range of their beers; for cider drinkers the choice is between Strongbow and Scrumpy Jack.

Dogs should remain in the garden – as should horses! (This is a favourite pub with those who ride on the hills.) The opening hours are 11 am to 3 pm and 6 pm to 11 pm Monday to Saturday and 12 noon to 3 pm and 7 pm to 10.30 pm on Sunday.

Telephone: 01562 883286.

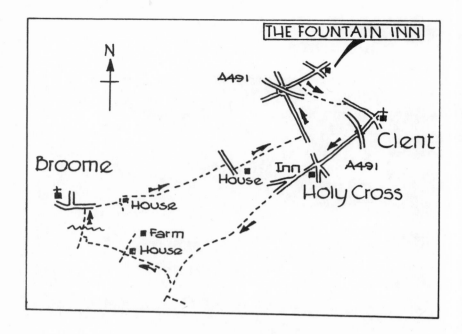

How to get there: From Hagley on the A456 take a lane signed to Clent. The inn is situated at a crossroads just before entering the village.

Parking: There is parking space at the front of the pub.

Length of the walk: 5½ miles. Map: OS Landranger series 139 Birmingham (inn GR 924797).

The walk is through gentle countryside below the slopes of the Clent Hills. Clent church has a fine 15th century tower with a huge clock; there is a more humble place of worship at Broome – the village takes its name from the shrub growing in a clearance in the Forest of Feckenham.

The Walk

From the car park cross to the lane signed to Broome. Within 400 yards take a signed path on the left. Walk through a rough pasture to a fence stile where there is also a township for many rabbits. Keep ahead through another rough pasture alongside a left-hand bushy hedge.

At the far end of the pasture the path is squeezed between fences to an old gateway and step stile. Now in a large meadow when you

50

see the church tower peeping over treetops bear left away from the main road to a rough stile in a gate. On a lane turn right to Clent village.

Turn right by the church. Follow the road under the main road to a road junction at Holy Cross. Cross to the third road left (just to the right of another inn). Within about ¼ mile and by railings take a lane going left. This is signed as a no through road.

The lane becomes a bridleway well used by horses. After 1½ miles climb a fence stile to an arable field on the right. (Note: if you reach a step stile – on left – or a main road you have missed the fence stile so retrace your steps.)

In the arable field walk directly away from the bridleway. When on the brow of the hill make for a gate just to the left of a house with distinctive Dutch gables. Cross a tarmac farm road to the signed path. Go over a stile and walk beside a left-hand hedge. In a far corner go around to the right a few steps to a stile.

Swing right in a pasture to cross a brook. Continue to a stile to a farm road at Broome. The church is to the left but you turn right. The farm road leads to a house and turns 90 degrees right. Here turn left along a tractor way then right around the house. The tractor way becomes a footpath and keeps a constant heading at the edge of fields to a lane. Turn right a few steps then take another path on the left.

Climb a bank and continue alongside a left-hand border with a house away to the right. The path leads to a lane. Turn left to a roundabout. Turn right to go under the main road. Rejoin the outward lane to return to the Fountain.

Drayton near **Belbroughton**
The Robin Hood

Drayton is a long way from Sherwood Forest but there was a sudden increase in pubs of this name when the Ancient Order of Foresters opened new courts or lodges in the 19th century. The age of the Robin Hood is deceptive from the outside; it looks fairly recent but has in fact served good fare for many years. As long ago as 1835 Henry Perrins bequeathed the building to his widow Hannah; the landlord around that time was Joseph Billingsley who held the licence for 30 years. There are two bars and one has a tiled floor made for the countryman's (and walker's) boots. The other is also cosy with its warm red carpets and furnishings, thick beams and inglenook fireplaces.

There is a comprehensive menu and specials listed on a board over the bar. I was attracted to the chicken Balinese Mexican spicy bake; my vegetarian friend enjoyed the broccoli cream cheese bake and we were tempted by such puds as walnut and butterscotch gateau. The choice of beers is between Ansells, Bass, and Ind Coope Burton Ale. Besides a good range of lagers there is draught Gaymer's Olde English Cyder. My border collie Nell stayed outside the pub along with the occupants of the seat marked for the sole use of the village idiots! This is a real family pub; children have their own menu and there is a magnificent adventure playground in the garden and plenty of space to chase and let off steam.

The opening hours are 12 noon to 2.30 pm and 6.30 pm to 11 pm Monday to Friday, with the same hours on Saturday except at lunchtime when the pub closes at 3 pm. Normal Sunday opening hours apply.

Telephone: 01562 730255.

How to get there: From Belbroughton on the B4188 take the lane south-west signed to Drayton. The inn is at the far end of the hamlet, just over the brook.

Parking: There is a car park at the side of the pub.

Length of the walk: 5½ miles. Map: OS Landranger series 139 Birmingham (inn GR 906758).

The walk is through a mixed countryside of arable and pastoral farming. There are several brooks which once powered scythe and sword mills. The footpaths over sown fields are not always reinstated but route finding should not prove difficult.

The Walk

From the car park turn right on the road. Drop down to the village shop and cross the brook. At once turn left along a lane. Within 300 yards and just past houses climb a stile on the left.

The footpath runs along the left-hand side of the field with the brook nearby on the left. You are never far from the stream as the path stays on a constant heading to a vehicle way. Continue to a lane. Turn right to climb out of the valley to a road junction.

Turn right. Within 400 yards the lane twists right. Here a path starts on the left. In a field walk by the left-hand edge to drop down to another brook and a cottage. Over the water maintain the heading across the field to a stile to the B4188. Cross the road to the signed path. Walk directly away from the road to climb a stile in the opposite boundary.

Bear right to a stile into a field which is often under the plough. Gain the right-hand border to a stile to a hard farm drive. Go directly over through a gate. Bear slightly right; over the brow make for a fence stile under a low tree.

On a bridleway turn right for a few steps. Climb a fence stile to a field left. The path now runs parallel to a right-hand road and climbs a stile adjoining a gate. Continue with a farm on the right side and walk

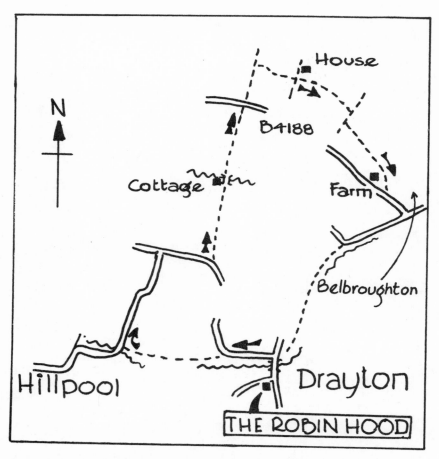

by a right-hand border of a pasture to a stile. There is then another to the road. Turn left.

Within ⅓ mile the road bends sharp left to the village of Belbroughton. At this point turn right along a lane bordering a stream and mill pools. As the lane twists right climb a stile. (The footpath sign may be broken.) The path is now clear beside a brook to the lane at Drayton. Turn left to the Robin Hood.

17 **Forhill** near **King's Norton**
The Peacock

The history of a pub on the site goes back several centuries but the present building dates from 1828 when, as part of the Weatheroak Estate, it was reconstructed as a hostelry for estate workers. The Estate was broken up and sold by auction in 1936; the pub was purchased by Cadbury's; this seems odd as they did not allow alcohol to be sold on their Bournville Estate. However, Cadbury's leased out the building and allowed the pub to reopen on condition that an adjoining tearoom be built which would be open at the same time as the licensed premises.

Today the Peacock is a delightful and rather different country pub. The furniture looks genuinely rustic and the floors are good red tiles – just right for walking boots and shoes. The constantly changing menu of home-cooked food, too (although standard dishes are available) tends to be a little different. Louise – through a door marked 'The Ferocious Cook' – was rather proud of her cucumber and prawn soup and herb crushed cod when I called. For vegetarians there was a Stilton quiche to enjoy. There is a special children's menu.

There is a great range of beers on offer, including Batham Bitter, Burton Bridge Bitter, Banks's, Hanson's Bitter and Mild, Marston's

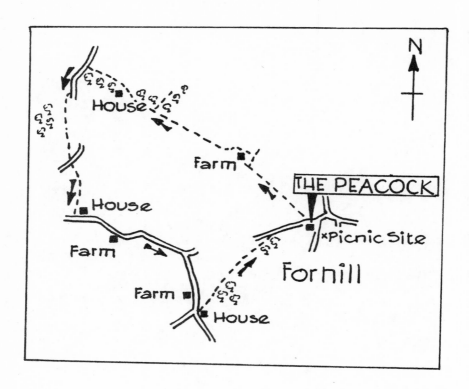

Bitter and Cameron's Ruby Red Bitter. There was also Judge's Bitter as a guest beer. The lager drinkers could enjoy the Czech Zamek Pilsner.

There are several linked bars (one where dogs are allowed) and the popular room is a smokeless zone. For milder days there are plenty of benches and tables on the neatly trimmed lawn. The opening hours are the normal weekday times but on Sundays food is served all day.

Telephone: 01564 823232.

How to get there: On the A441 at the city boundary at West Heath take a lane to Wythall on the left. The Peacock is signed after 2 miles on the right.

Parking: There is a car park opposite the pub.

Length of the walk: 4 miles. Map: OS Landranger series 139 Birmingham (inn GR 054755).

Forhill is high on the Wast Hills. The Council have sited a picnic site here which overlooks the Worcestershire countryside. The North Worcestershire Path runs by the pub and the walk is through a pastoral landscape and fine woods.

The Walk

From the car park turn right along the lane then at once right again along a vehicle way signed as a footpath. Within almost ½ mile go over a stile to the right. At once in a pasture swing left to keep a farmstead on the left side.

Keep ahead along a waymarked route to join a tarmac vehicle drive. Maintain the direction. Just before the garden and gates of a house the path goes off to the right. Follow the track through the trees to a stile to a field. Keep the direction to a lane.

Turn left; within a few steps and where the lane bears left take a signed path on the right. The right of way is almost parallel to the lane then goes into the next field (sometimes arable) to a lane. Climb a stile almost opposite to sheep pastures. Follow the path to emerge over a stile onto a lane just to the right of a house.

Turn left along the lane. Bear right at a junction. At the next junction a path starts over a stile left of a house. Climb the bank to another stile. In a meadow walk by a right-hand wood to a stile alongside a gate. Maintain the heading to a stile on a bank. Still keep the direction along the left-hand border of a field. Further stiles show the way to walk near a house and garden to enter a wood. Follow the winding track to a stile and over to a lane. The Peacock is about 400 yards to the right.

18 Long Lawford
The Lawford Arms

This is a cosy and completely unpretentious pub, it has a simplicity which appeals to me – especially after a walk when one does not have to be too concerned about muddy boots or a tired dog. Both are welcomed in the continuous bar which has plenty of stone-flagged floors. There is no fancy food here, although the baps with ample and tasty fillings are typical bar fare.

Interesting rural characters are to be found – one recounted to me the tale of the pub's ghost, a lady who props herself up in the corner by the fire. There was a murder up at Lawford Hall in the late 18th century when Sir Theodosius Broughton was poisoned by Captain Donnellan.

The Lawford Arms is a pub for games – there are darts, quizzes, pool, football and bar skittles and always interesting chat – except perhaps when a live band visits! The beer choice at this freehouse is between Brew XI and Bass; Caffreys is popular as is the draught Blackthorn cider. This pub is willing to welcome ramblers all day from Monday to Saturday; Sunday, of course, has to conform to the normal restricted opening hours.

Telephone: 01788 571889.

How to get there: Long Lawford is 3 miles west of Rugby just off the A428. Turn right along Chapel Street. Immediately over the railway turn right (Railway Street) then first left. The Lawford Arms is a few yards along Main Street on the left.

Parking: You may park behind the pub or in the street.

Length of the walk: 5 miles. Map: OS Landranger series 140 Leicester and Coventry (inn GR 472759).

The walk is through the pleasant countryside of the upper Avon valley. Much of these lands was once owned by the Benedictine order of Monks Kirby. When Henry VIII dissolved the monasteries the Broughton family were rewarded with the lordship of the manor in 1542. Along a lane the route goes near the site of Newnham Regis Baths. An attempt was made to use the saline springs and create a spa to rival Leamington Spa. You can also see a church tower in a farmyard. This was once part of St Lawrence's church.

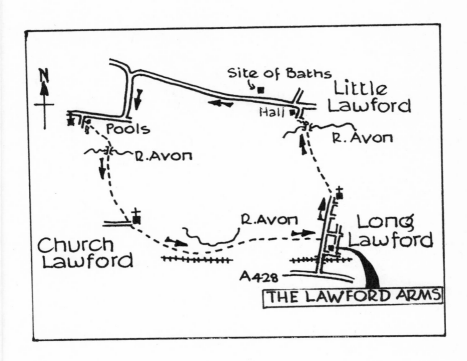

The Walk

Out of the pub turn right then right again (Railway Street). At a T-junction turn right down Chapel Street. At the very end there is a bridleway signed at the side of a house drive.

Follow the track through a gate and meadows. The bridleway goes over the river and along a causeway to a farm. Go through the farmyard and along the drive. Swing right by the ford to pass the old Hall which bears the date 1604. At a junction of lanes turn left and pass the site (on the right) of the old baths.

Bear left at a junction then keep on the lane to King's Newnham. Reach another road junction where you will see the lofty church tower in its farmyard setting; it was a ruin until it was re-roofed by the Duke of Buccleuch in 1900.

Turn left at the junction then at once left again through a bridlegate. Take a note of the arrowed direction. Walk by pools (stew ponds made to supply fresh fish to the monks of Kenilworth Abbey) then over the meadow (on that noted direction) to a bridge. Continue across the river Avon. The path is now clear over fields.

Climb out of the valley along an avenue of small saplings to a rough step stile. At once climb another stile then head towards a church tower over a field. The church is at Church Lawford and much of it was rebuilt in 1872. Follow the signed footpath through the church-yard keeping to the right of the church. Climb a stile to a meadow. Follow the indicated direction to another stile and maintain the heading to a bend in the river Avon.

Now walking parallel to the right-hand railway maintain a constant heading to pick up a left-hand hedge. Beyond gates go over a bridge across a stream. Keep ahead to a stile between houses. On a road at Long Lawford turn right, this is Chapel Street again. Retrace your steps to the pub.

Brandon
The Royal Oak

This is a pub for the beer enthusiast who wants to know more about his favourite brew; apart from the malt sacks and assorted barrels as decorative features, there are numerous interesting prints and photographs about the ancient art of brewing, examples of old cellar tools and even types of malts used. Home brewing was an important aspect in the history of the Royal Oak. In 1850 Mrs Sarah Cave is listed as a beer retailer, followed by her son Tom who became licensee of the Royal Oak 'and refreshment room in Brandon' and also 'brewer and maltster'. The final mention of the brewing is in 1921. Today this is an Ansells pub, and there are also Tetley beers available besides a good range of ciders and lagers.

This is one of Ansells 'Big Steak' pubs so there is a daunting choice of food on the standard menu (including a monster 2 lb steak!). There is a good choice for vegetarians with at least three dishes and the cold salad platters looked especially attractive. There is a huge specials board above the bar; on my visit the Indonesian hot and sour chicken was tempting.

The opening hours are 11.30 am to 3 pm and 5.30 pm to 11 pm Monday to Saturday and usual hours on a Sunday. Outside is a

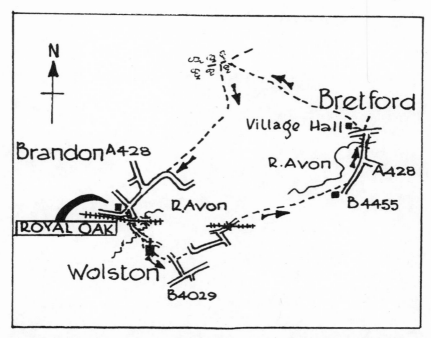

magnificent play area for youngsters where the equipment has good safety features. There are also plenty of benches and tables for those fine sunny days.
Telephone: 01203 542304.

How to get there: Brandon is just off the A428, 5 miles east of Coventry. The Royal Oak is by the prominent railway line that marks the border of the village.

Parking: There are two car parks; one is beside the pub and the other across the road.

Length of the walk: 4 miles. Map: OS Landranger series 140 Leicester and Coventry (inn GR 761409).

The route is through the valley of the river Avon. The hamlet of Brandon is divided from the larger village of Wolston by a main line railway. The church at Wolston is said to have 'something of nearly every century from Conqueror's day to ours'. The manor house was dismantled about the time of the First World War and taken to America for rebuilding. The castle too has gone — probably destroyed by Simon de Montfort in a battle in about 1266.

The Walk

Go along the road under the railway bridge to enter Wolston. Continue to a footbridge over the Avon. Alongside are the weather-worn stones of the four-arched roadbridge. Follow the path through gates right to St Margaret's church. Turn left.

Join the vehicle way soon alongside a bubbling eager tributary of the Avon. Cross over a cattle grid and continue to a road. Cross and walk down the path by the Old Post Office to an estate road. Keep ahead along Meadow Road.

At the end (T-junction) turn left then right at another T-junction. (Nearby is the Priory — this is of uncertain age — perhaps 1640 — and was probably an offshoot of the Cistercian Coombe Abbey.)

Walk under a railway and over a cattle grid. Follow the vehicle track past the house and by barns. The waymarked way leads (never far from the river on the left) to a house drive and a road (the Romans' Fosse Way). Turn left over the river using the 500 year old bridge. At a junction in the village of Bretford turn left.

Within a few steps turn right down a bridleway marked by a blue arrow. (Note this is not the signed bridleway actually on the road junction.) The vehicle way soon bends to the village hall but we keep straight ahead along a bold track to pass through a broken bridlegate. The route is well used by horses and climbs sharply then there is a fenced way along the borders of fields.

Keep ahead through a metal hunting gate with the fenced way still clear. Join another wide track and bear left to walk through an elongated wood. After about 200 yards turn left through a gateway (no gate).

The track is waymarked (blue arrow on post) alongside a left-hand hedge. There is a clear track to the A428. Maintain the direction along the main road. On entering Brandon the main road twists sharp right. Here keep ahead along a one-way street which goes to the pub.

20 Wildmoor
The Wildmoor Oak

This is called 'The Inn on the Stream' – the brook is one of the many that tumble off the Lickey Hills, and though rather isolated from main roads the Wildmoor Oak offers excellent hospitality, as is evidenced by its popularity. All the food is home-made with the emphasis on English fare. The Oak drunken casseroles looked delicious and I was told that the steak and kidney was 'by far the best in the area'. Prices are very reasonable and children have their own menu which includes the intriguing dinosaur fish dish. There are usually about half a dozen choices for vegetarians.

All the range of Bass beers are available besides Caffreys and several lagers. The choice of draught ciders is between Taunton's Dry Blackthorn and Autumn Gold. The chief feature of the gardens is the many old sinks and baths overflowing not with water but with tumbling flowers and colourful shrubs. There are plenty of benches and tables and this is the place to leave Fido.

The history of the pub is not clear, although it is certainly old as it features on the first issue of OS maps. It must surely have been a quiet retreat for local agricultural workers in days gone by. There is much quaint memorabilia on the walls (and ceilings!) of the bar: plates, jugs, mugs and vehicle number plates are sent from many countries of the world – there is something to stimulate everyone's conversation.

The hours when food is served at this rather special pub are 12 noon to 2 pm and 6.30 pm to 9.30 pm Monday to Saturday and 12 noon to 2.30 pm and 7 pm to 9 pm on Sunday. Normal pub hours are in force around these times.

Telephone: 0121 453 2696.

How to get there: Go ¾ mile north-westwards along the A491 from Junction 4 of the M5. Turn left along a lane. Within ¼ mile there is a crossroads. The Wildmoor Oak is a few yards to the right.

Parking: There are car parks opposite and at the side of the pub.

Length of the walk: 4½ miles. Map: OS Landranger series 139 Birmingham (inn GR 964755).

The pub nestles below the Lickey Hills; the walk climbs to the lovely heights which now comprise a country park. There are several sand pits near the inn; these are a valuable source of fuller's earth which is widely used for industrial and medicinal purposes.

The Walk

From the crossroads near the pub walk along the lane to the A491. Cross directly over to a stile and signed footpath. In a pasture walk near the left-hand willowed border. In a far corner go through a gate and at once swing right to walk under the motorway.

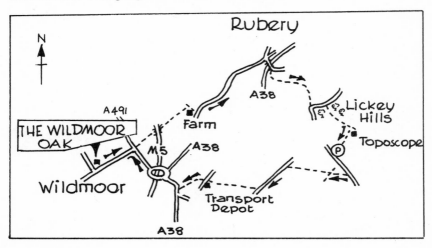

At the end of the long tunnel go over a stile. Follow the arrowed direction to walk through fields aiming to the left of a farmhouse. Follow a way by barns to reach a farm drive. Turn right to a lane. Turn left.

The narrow lane climbs and passes the entrance to a country park. A few steps beyond is a road junction. Turn right to go across a bridge over a main highway. Immediately over take a signed bridleway along a wide track on the right. This leads to a lane.

Turn left; after a few yards turn right along a path signed on the right. This leads through woods then along a grassed way above the scarp edge (on left) of the Lickey Hills. Follow a way to a castle-like structure (a toposcope). Turn right over the grass to walk through a car park to a lane.

Turn left. Within 200 yards the next path starts on the right. The way is well walked and clear over the field to cross a house drive. Maintain the heading over fields and stiles to a lane. Turn left.

Within ½ mile take a path over a stile on the right. In the field walk alongside the right-hand hedge. Maintain the direction to walk alongside a transport depot to a lane. Cross to the path over a stile opposite. Go alongside the right-hand border of a rough meadow to a rather concealed stile to a farm vehicle track. Keep the old direction to a main road.

Turn right. Cross a roundabout then continue along the A491. Within 400 yards turn down a lane left to retrace your steps to the pub.

Warings Green near **Hockley Heath**
The Blue Bell Cider House

21

For many years this famous pub alongside the Stratford-upon-Avon Canal made its own cider from locally grown apples. Today serious cider drinkers still come to this rather isolated pub for the splendid range on offer but the drink is now all bought-in. Choose from Strongbow, Bulmer's, Scrumpy Jack, Max Dry Strong White and Bulmer's Original. The beer drinkers are not forgotten with Foster's, John Smith's Bitter, Chestnut Mild, Ruddles, Beamish Stout, Kronenbourg and Kaliber Alcohol Free.

This is a traditional pub with cosy corners for that quiet chat. The walls have old photographs of days long past which will stimulate any flagging conversation. Although children are not allowed in the bars, that is not to say they are not welcome: there is a conservatory where they can eat and the garden where there are benches and play equipment. There is a children's menu and a junior menu for more ravenous youngsters. There is also a separate OAP menu for lunchtime and evening with advantageous prices. The food offered at the Blue Bell is very varied but I especially liked the sound of the jacket potatoes with a choice of six fillings and the Yorkshire puddings with five accompaniments.

The hours of opening are from 11.30 am to 3 pm and 5.30 pm to 11 pm Monday to Friday. Saturday has all-day opening and there are the normal Sunday hours (12 noon to 3 pm and 7 pm to 10.30 pm). Fido will have to remain outside at all hours, I'm afraid.
Telephone: 01564 702328.

How to get there: Take the B4102 from Shirley. Within 2 miles cross a canal bridge. Immediately turn left along a lane then bear left at a junction. The Blue Bell is ½ mile further.

Parking: There is a car park at the side of the pub.

Length of the walk: 5 miles. Map: OS Landranger series 139 Birmingham (inn GR 129742).

The walk starts along the Stratford Canal which was built about 200 years ago to convey coal southwards and lime in the other direction. Later the route is around Earlswood reservoir; two brooks were dammed to give a water supply to the canal. Now the expanse of water delights anglers and yachtsmen as well as walkers and nature lovers.

The Walk

Out of the car park turn right along the lane and cross the waterway. At once go through a little gate on the right to give access to the canal towpath.

Turn right and continue with the water on the left side. There is now a pleasant stretch of canalside walking where ducks scurry as you approach. At the second roadbridge gain the road and turn left. Keep ahead past a junction and inn to a crossroads. Go straight over (Wood Lane).

The lane passes a farm where delicious ices are sold. At the start of a wood on the left a path starts at the far side of a little car park. Go through a kissing-gate and turn left to a meadow. Follow the right-hand border alongside a wood. Go through a far gap and keep just to the right of a youth organisation hut, walking alongside a wood fence.

Bear right by a 'Private Property' notice. Walk along a well-defined track with open fields to the left to a railed bridge over a brook. Across the water turn right. The reeded reservoir is on the left side. The track bears left around the end of the reservoir. Pass by a railed bridge.

Still alongside the reservoir keep along the well-used track to a crossing path. Turn right over a railed bridge. Walk through a car park to a road.

Turn right then left along a vehicle drive signed as a path. Walk along the end of another reservoir then continue to a road. Turn right

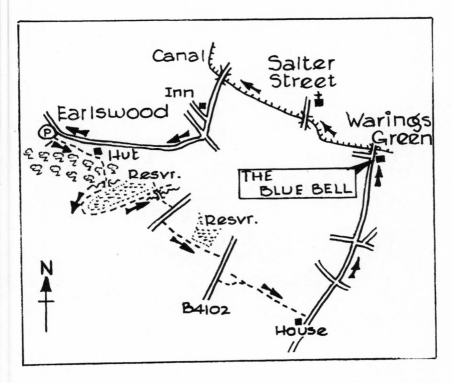

for ¼ mile. By bungalow numbered 124 turn left along a path signed through a little gate. Walk along a vehicle way to a stile to a field.

Bear left to a vehicle drive. Turn right along the drive. Climb a rather obsolete stile beside a gate and keep on this heading through fields to a lane. Turn left. Go over a crossroads. The lane leads to the pub.

22 Dodford
The Dodford Inn

Refurbished in recent years, this Victorian inn in a quiet spot is well worth seeking out for its excellent prices. There were twelve main dishes for a few pounds when I called with even keener prices for Senior Citizens at lunchtime. Children and vegetarians have not been forgotten either. This Greenalls house has been meticulously refurbished with a terrace overlooking a beautiful wooded valley where there is a picnic spot and where visitors' tents and caravans can be sited.

There is one bar with green decor which complements the woodland views. There are interesting prints and displays of cigarette cards on the walls and the dartboard invites friendly competition – the pub is still looking for a darts team! There are Greenalls Original, Bitter and Mild beers and Tetley is also available. The choice of ciders is between Strongbow, Woodpecker and Scrumpy Jack. This is one of those pubs where opening hours are flexible.

Telephone: 01527 832470.

How to get there: 2 miles west of Bromsgrove turn right along a lane signed to Dodford. After ½ mile take a lane left to pass the church. Go right at a T-junction. The pub is signed 400 yards on the right.

Parking: There is a large car park alongside the pub.

Length of the walk: 4 miles. Map: OS Landranger series 139 Birmingham (inn GR 939729).

The walk is around the village of Dodford. This was to have been a Chartist village of 4-acre smallholdings in the last century and the straight roads were built. The idealist's dreams came to naught when there were severe financial problems. There are paths through mixed farmland and woods and alongside clear brooks.

The Walk
From the car park climb a corner stile and follow the arrowed direction down steps to the valley. Swing right by the picnic area to continue with a stream on the left. Join a vehicle way to a lane. (Near here was the site of Dodford Priory but little remains today.)

Cross the lane to climb a stile to a pasture. Maintain the old heading to climb to a vehicle drive. Still keep the direction along the tarmac way. When this twists sharp right still keep ahead along a path to drop down the valley. Cross a brook to enter a wood.

When the clear path divides take the right-hand way. The track twists through the trees to meet a vehicle way by a house. Turn right (house now on right side) and continue along a bridleway to a lane. Turn right. At a road junction turn right.

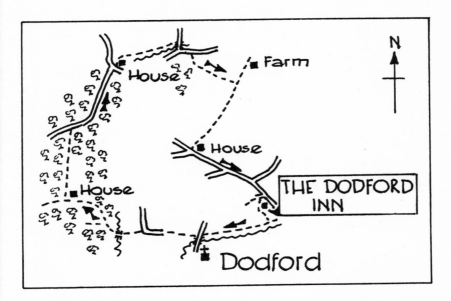

Within a few steps a path is signed on the left. Go through a metal gate then walk alongside right-hand barns and a pool where ducks glide. Through two further gates follow the arrowed direction to follow a right-hand brook to a lane. Turn right then left at a junction. After 150 yards take a signed path over a stile right. At another stile two paths are indicated. Take the way signed ahead over a pasture to another stile.

Maintain the direction to reach a bridleway to the right of a farmstead. Turn right and continue to a lane. Turn left. Within ¾ mile turn right down Whinfield Road to the pub.

23 Barnt Green
The Barnt Green Inn

This Grade II listed building is another of those buildings which was never intended to be a hostelry when constructed but which now makes a splendid refreshment house. It was a 15th century manor house owned by the Windsor-Clives who were land agents to the earls of Plymouth; it remained as a residence until auctioned in 1964. There are stories of a tunnel between the old house and Cofton church, but I had my doubts when I looked at the map – the distance is a good mile! I am also a little sceptical about the ghost of a drummer boy who was incarcerated in the tunnel. From such theories are bar room stories fashioned!

There are several comfortable linked bars. The range of beers is from Bass and M & B breweries and the lager choice is between Carling Pilsner, Tennents and Caffreys. Besides the à la carte menu there are square meal deals which offer up to three courses at a fixed price. Families and children are welcome and they can choose between the young Toby fare if 7 years and under or the special children's menu if 12 and under – all with chips and baked beans. Vegetarians on my visit could select either vegetable tikka masala or savoury broccoli and brie.

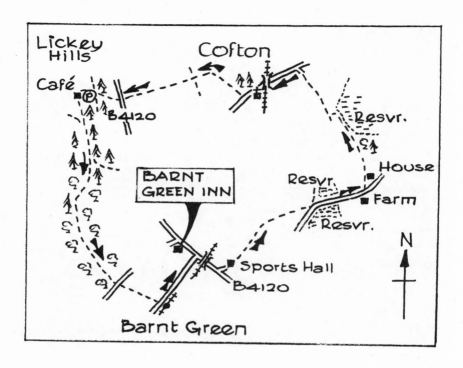

This building of many gables is set in pleasant grounds where there are plenty of tables and benches. Nell my border collie had to admire the flowers rather than the inside decor. The opening times are 12 noon to 2.30 pm and 5.30 pm to 11 pm Monday to Saturday and normal Sunday hours of 12 noon to 3 pm and 6 pm to 10.30 pm.
Telephone: 0121 445 4949.

How to get there: The pub is on the B4120, 1 mile south of the city boundary on the right-hand side on entering the village.

Parking: There is parking at the front and rear of the pub.

Length of the walk: 4 miles. Map: OS Landranger series 139 Birmingham (inn GR 007741).

The route is over a mixed countryside of wooded heathland and farmland. Lanes and paths go between the two Bittell reservoirs which were constructed to 'top up' the water in the nearby canal. These areas of water are a haven for large numbers of wildfowl.

The Walk

From the car parks walk to the main road. Turn right and go under a railway bridge. At once turn left down the cul-de-sac of Margesson Drive.

At the far end and behind a sports hall climb a stile. In a pasture walk alongside the left-hand hedge. Go into the next field and bear right to the far diagonal corner passing near a wooded depression. Climb a stile to a lane. Turn left and climb the rise passing a reservoir.

Within 300 yards and just before a house take the footpath over a stile on the left. Continue near the right-hand boundary and climb the wooded rise. Go over a stile and walk along the dam of another reservoir.

At the end swing left to climb a stile to a vehicle way. Turn right. At a junction of ways turn left along a lane. Go under a railway and past the little 600 year old Cofton church. A few steps further and by a wood take a signed path on the right. The track goes away from the lane then bears left to cross a hard path.

Keep ahead through sheep pastures and near the right-hand boundary to stiles to the B4120. Cross to the path opposite. Climb the ridge. Bear right then left to an information chalet and café. Turn left and walk along a path with a children's play area away to the right.

Keep ahead when a wide vehicle way joins our path. Maintain the direction (not to the left) when the track divides. Follow the wide way through woods to a lane. Cross to the opposite path which leads to a road. Turn left to the B4120. The pub is to the left.

Lapworth
The Punch Bowl

The new Punch Bowl replaces a humble little pub for agricultural workers which burnt down a few years ago. Inside there are original old beams, exposed brickwork and an olde world ambience combined with modern amenities. The full range of Banks's ales are available and how good to see good house wines (Chardonnay) at reasonable prices. From the kitchen come dishes such as avocado with bacon, flash fried liver and salmon roulade besides popular standard fare. How good too to see my favourite forbidden pudding, spotted dick, on offer. There are always goodies available for vegetarians. Families are encouraged and there are play areas and a special menu for children. No dogs inside, please.

The opening hours are 11.30 am to 3 pm Monday to Friday. On Saturday the pub fare is available all day. There are the normal hours on Sunday.

Telephone: 01564 784564.

How to get there: Go eastwards along the B4439 from Hockley Heath. Take the third lane left after 2 miles. Bear right when the lane divides. The Punch Bowl is ¾ mile further.

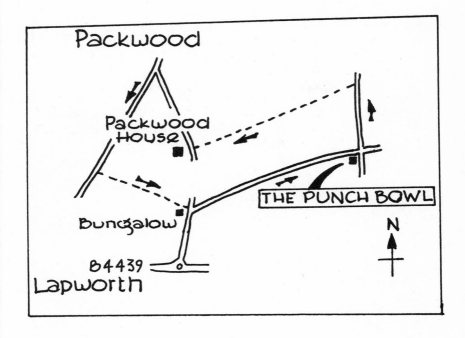

Parking: There is a car park behind the pub.

Length of the walk: 2½ miles. Map: OS Landranger series 139 Birmingham (inn GR 184720).

On this walk the National Trust gem of Packwood House is visited. Besides the interesting mansion (which started life as a farmhouse in about 1560) there is the 17th century Yew Garden which represents the Sermon on the Mount.

The Walk

The inn is on a crossroads. Go over to Chessetts Wood Road. Within ⅓ mile climb a stile on the left to Packwood Avenue and the National Trust grounds of Packwood House. The path goes along the avenue of lovely oak trees.

The straight path leads directly to a lane. Turn right to pass the gabled Packwood House. After ¼ mile there is a road junction. Turn left along Grove Lane. The shady lane leads past a rather fine disused gateway to a signed path on the left.

Climb a stile to parkland where sheep graze. Follow the arrowed direction. There is a fine view of the rear of Packwood House across a lake. In the parkland keep near the right-hand border and pass a waymark post. The path leads to a fence stile to an often sown field.

Walk along the border then turn round the corner. Look for a rather concealed stile. Go along a plank causeway and keep ahead to the next stile. Maintain the direction at the side of a pasture then keep just to the left of a bungalow.

Continue along the edge of the lawns with a pool on the left side to a stile to a lane at a junction. Walk along Rising Lane (signed to Baddesley Clinton). On the ¾ mile back to the Punch Bowl you pass elegant houses with their appropriately elegant gardens.

Wroxall
㉕ The Case is Altered

It is pretty safe to say that there is not another inn so-called throughout
the land; the explanations are many and varied but the one favoured
by the licensee's granddaughter is that a past publican wanted a spirits
licence. This was at first refused by the justices but allowed on appeal.
Others say that some 250 years ago there was a baker here. His
application to have a brewer's licence was rejected. He also took his
pleas to a higher court and 'the case was altered'.

Whatever the origins, this is a quaint freehouse which is popular
with ramblers. They are not allowed in the carpeted lounge wearing
boots but are welcomed in the stone-flagged bar. There are heavy
beams and supports and small windows which give an especial snug
feeling on a winter's day. You can sit around the small tables and find
many artefacts to stimulate conversation. There is, for example, a
display sign for a long defunct brewery at Leamington – I had never
heard of Lucas, Blackwell and Arkwright ales. No food is served here
except sandwiches in the summer months. However, there is a good
selection of beer including Flowers Original, Ansells Traditional Bitter
and Mild and Samuel Smith's.

Outside there is a small terrace at the rear. Here you can sit and

admire the hanging baskets and roses which climb high to the eaves. This small old pub is not really suitable for children or dogs. The hours of opening are 11.30 am to 2.30 pm Monday to Saturday and 12 noon to 2 pm and 7 pm to 10.30 pm on Sunday.
Telephone: 01926 484206.

How to get there: At the Five Ways Roundabout (5 miles north of Warwick along the A4141) turn left (signed Shrewley) then at once right along Case Lane. The pub is within 400 yards on the left.

Parking: There is a car park at the rear of the pub.

Length of the walk: 3½ miles. Map: OS Landranger series 139 Birmingham (inn GR 224701).

The route is through Hay Wood — an extensive area of mixed trees which are particularly attractive in springtime. On the return leg the path passes near Wroxall Abbey. Originally the home of Benedictine nuns, it was founded in 1135 but all we can see now of that establishment is the ancient church and parts of the cloisters. There was once an Elizabethan house nearby which was bought by Sir Christopher Wren when he was over 80. This house was replaced by a Victorian mansion which now houses a school.

The Walk

Follow the lane left out of the car park. Bear right at a junction. Within 400 yards there is a wide tractor entrance to gates on the right. Here a path is signed over a stile. Follow the arrowed way in a pasture alongside a left-hand hedge.

Within 50 yards climb a stile left. Two paths are signed here; take the left-hand way. The route is now waymarked through fields with lovely woods away to the right. In a large field take the direction well to the right of the row of trees on the crown of the hill (somewhat to the right of the arrowed direction).

In the far corner of the field go through a metal gate. Turn right along the lane and within a step or two turn left at a junction. After ¾ mile look for a signed bridleway on the right. This is part of the long distance pathway, the Heart of England Way and the route is well arrowed to a church drive at Baddesley Clinton. You go right but left is the church of St Michael with its tower built about 1500. Also left is the splendid moated Hall (now owned by the National Trust).

The church drive leads to a lane. Turn left then at once right along the drive to a cottage. Go through a gate and follow the marked track through the trees. Out of the woods make for a group of farm buildings across a pasture. Follow the drive to the main road. Turn

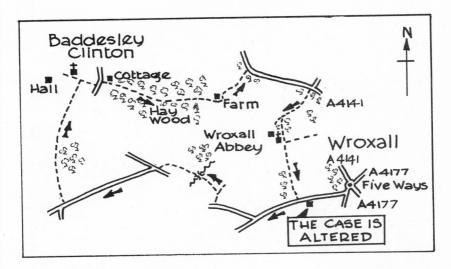

right. Within ¾ mile and by a drive go over a stile to parkland on the right.

Follow the drive; after 300 yards bear left along an avenue of trees. Go through a gate to a tarmac drive. Walk alongside a right-hand wall and keep ahead (Wroxall Abbey on right). When the main drive goes left maintain the old direction to walk through sheep pastures (woods on right) and continue to a stile to a lane. The Case is Altered is a step or two to the left.

26 Kenilworth
The Queen and Castle

This attractive Beefeater house maintains an excellent reputation for good value for money, and I am sure that behind the ivy-clad exterior there lurks a wonderful history. But no one, either pub staff or the locals, could enlighten me. Perhaps because of the proximity of one of the finest castles in the land – a place with a well-documented history – no one bothers about the past days of the pub! It looks to date from about three centuries ago, with ancient beams and exposed brickwork inside. There is dimmed lighting in the bar and restaurant and many divisions provide cosy niches to discuss the highlights of the walk. (I think the pub was once popular with cyclists as there is an old National Cyclists Union plaque on the wall.)

The good range of beers includes Boddingtons Bitter, Flowers Original, Wadworth's 6X and Whitbread's Trophy. The choice for lager lovers is Heineken or Stella Artois and cider drinkers have draught Strongbow or Woodpecker. There is the usual large range of Beefeater dishes on the menu with separate 'Younger Discoveries' dishes and also the Mr Men children's menu. In addition there is a specials board behind the bar. No dogs is the rule in this pub.

The pub is open all day but with the usual restricted Sunday hours. Telephone: 01926 52661.

How to get there: Follow the signs for Kenilworth Castle. The pub is opposite the castle at Castle Green on the B4103.

Parking: There is a large car park at the side of the pub.

Length of the walk: 8 miles. Map: OS Landranger series 139 Birmingham and 140 Leicester and Coventry (inn GR 280723).

The pub is overlooked by the magnificent ruin of Kenilworth Castle. Kenilworth, which witnessed so much of the changing history of the land, was merely a clearing called Chinewede at the time of the Domesday Survey in 1086. It was in 1122 that Henry I gave the rocky outcrop to his treasurer Geoffrey de Clinton. He decided the site was ideal to build a home worthy of his position. Henry II declared it was too opulent for a commoner and took over the place. The days of the castle's glory lasted for 400 years, only to end after the termination of the Civil War in 1649.

The Walk
From the pub cross the road towards the castle and turn right. Within a few steps turn left down Purlieu Road. Cross a brook (which once filled the castle moat and huge defensive lake). Climb a stile on the right and follow the arrowed direction. Pass barns and walk over fields to a lane.

Turn left. Walk along a farm road for about 1 mile. Just past a wood on the left turn left along a wide farm track. The track drops down to a junction of ways. Turn right.

Follow the waymarked route which crosses a brook then emerges on a lane by Honiley church. (The building dates from 1723 and may

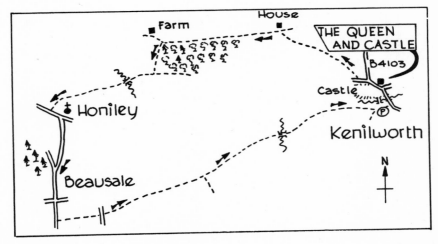

have been designed by Sir Christopher Wren who lived a mile or so away at Wroxall.) Turn left then right along the lane.

Maintain the direction at road junctions; a few hundred yards past the second junction take a signed path down a vehicle drive left. Go over a stile and continue to a lane. Cross directly over along a cart track. When this swings left maintain the old direction.

You soon see the gaunt distant silhouette of the castle and the path towards it is well waymarked. The route crosses Inchford Brook – another stream which fed the castle lake. Near the castle climb a stile and go a few steps right to a vehicle way by a car park. Walk left along the vehicle way then left again along the wide way over the old moat.

Immediately before the entrance to the castle go down steps right. Walk alongside left-hand railings then the castle walls. Continue to a kissing-gate to the road by the Queen and Castle.

Rowington
The Cock Horse

The publican told me that this had been a pub for 400 years so it is crammed full of character. It was once a forge but the cock horse was kept on the premises to assist pulling the carriages up the steep hill into Rowington. In those days this was the main road from Warwick to Birmingham so there was plenty of business for the horse.

There is a fine menu at reasonable prices – traditional Sunday lunch for example at less than a fiver. If I were a vegetarian I am sure I would go for the vegetable Mexicana – broccoli and cauliflower in a spicy tomato sauce. In addition to the standard menu there is always a specials board. There is a homely-looking beamed bar and a comfortable dining room with a lovely blazing log fire in the inglenook fireplace on chilly days. The beers sold are Boddingtons Bitter, Flowers IPA and Flowers Original. The cider drinkers can use traditional ceramic mugs.

Outside there are plenty of tables and benches overlooking the open countryside. Well-supervised children are allowed inside the pub but I'm sorry Fido – you remain outside and admire the view. Opening hours are 12 noon to 2.30 pm and 6 pm to 11 pm Monday to Saturday. Sunday hours are 12 noon to 3 pm and 7 pm to 10.30 pm.

Telephone: 01926 842183.

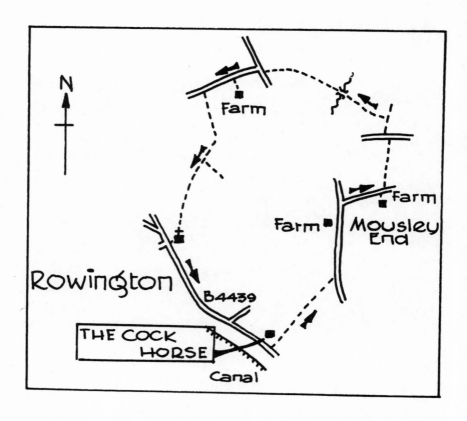

How to get there: Rowington is on the Old Warwick Road between Warwick and Hockley Heath. The Cock Horse is on the right just before the village.

Parking: There are car parks to the front and rear of the pub.

Length of the walk: 3 miles. Map: OS Landranger series 139 Birmingham (inn GR 209688).

The walk is over mixed arable and pastoral farmland around the village of Rowington. This was once a village where members of the Shakespeare family lived. The 14th century tower of the church of St Lawrence looks out over the valley. Across a field from the return road is a high bank. It is rather strange to see boats moving along the high bank – the Grand Union Canal (which was formed in 1929 by joining many small waterways) is here.

The Walk

Out of the car park turn left along the B4439. Within a step or two a signed path starts through a metal gate on the left. Take the arrowed direction through a pasture. In the far left corner climb a stile then go over a plank bridge to the adjoining field. At once turn right to continue by a right-hand hedge.

Climb a fence stile to a lane. Turn left. Climb a hill then bear right (signed Mousley End) at a junction. Within 300 yards take a signed path over a stile on the left. Take the indicated heading. Pass into the next field and walk by right-hand hedges to a lane. Turn left then at once right over a stile by a metal gate.

Walk by the hedge left to climb a stile. Follow the arrowed way left to walk above a ditch to a gateway and stile. Keep the old heading alongside a left-hand hedge to a corner stile and footbridge. Now in a very large field make for the very far right corner.

Go through a metal gate. Turn right on the lane then immediately left. Within ⅓ mile take a signed path through a gate left. Cross a pasture to the opposite stile. Maintain the direction to where the corner of an adjoining field juts into our field. Bear right to a gateway. Here two paths are signed. Keep the old direction. Stiles and waymarks show the way to the churchyard of Rowington church. Keep to the right of the church and walk down steps to the road. The pub is to the left.

28 Bubbenhall
The Malt Shovel

Over four centuries ago this popular community pub was the Court House; the history also reveals that here was the brewhouse for another pub. Not only is it a place for refreshment but also as a focus for several sports teams, including darts and a successful football team. There is also a pub bowling rink – what better than a gentle game after your walk.

All the food at the Malt Shovel is home-produced; the range is wide but Italian dishes are prominent, including an excellent tagliatelli carbonara. Vegetarians are not especially catered for but there will always be a dish or two to suit. Children have their favourites – mostly with chips and beans of course!

There is a good range of beers including brews from Bass, Ansells and Tetley and there is always a guest beer on offer – when I called it was Young's – up from London!

This is a rural pub where my collie Nell was welcomed into the bar by Meg – the Heinz 57/King Charles spaniel. The tiled floor of the bar also tolerates walking boots; the lounge is a different matter, here there is a warm pinky glow from the carpet and decor and an open fire is a welcoming feature.

The opening hours are 11.30 am to 3 pm and 6 pm to 11 pm Monday to Saturday and the normal 12 noon to 3 pm and 7 pm to 10.30 pm on Sundays. Meals hours are shorter.
Telephone: 01203 301141.

How to get there: The pub is just off the A445 south of Coventry. Take the lane through the village. Just before Church Road the Malt Shovel is down a cul-de-sac on the right.

Parking: There is a car park behind the pub.

Length of the walk: 7 miles. Map: OS Landranger series 140 Leicester and Coventry (inn GR 363725).

The triangular walk links three small villages and crosses two rivers. Stoneleigh is now renowned for the National Agricultural Centre and Royal Showground in the old lands of the Cistercian Abbey. The Abbey was established in 1154 but was destroyed by fire a century later; Henry III assisted in the reconstruction. A restored Roman fort can be seen at Baginton and Bubbenhall's church is 13th century and overlooks the Avon.

The Walk

Out of the car park turn left then right at a T-junction. Within a step or two turn right down Church Road. Go through the gate at the end to walk through the churchyard. Keep the church on the right to pass through a kissing-gate to a field. Follow the signed direction keeping parallel to the right-hand fence. Maintain the direction through a pasture then follow the path to a road.

Turn right. Within 400 yards there is a junction. Bear right along the lane signed to Baginton. We pass over the ancient bridge and keep on this way to Baginton. At the start of the village and just past an inn take a lane on the left (but the restored Roman fort is ¼ mile further). Turn left down Church Road. At the end of the road is the church of St John Baptist. (Just east of the building was Baginton Castle; it nudged the river but little remains today except a few earthworks and ridges.)

Turn left down a signed pathway. Go by cottages and pass through a gate and cross a brook. Go over a stile to a meadow and bear right then follow the path near the river Sowe to bridges over the water to the B4113. Turn left to Stoneleigh.

Turn right to the little village green with its old blacksmith's workshop (dated 1851). Bear left (blacksmith on right) alongside the Alice Leigh Almshouses. The Leighs were the Lords of the Manor at Stoneleigh and built the almshouses in 1594.

Turn left to the Norman church. Follow the path (keep to the right

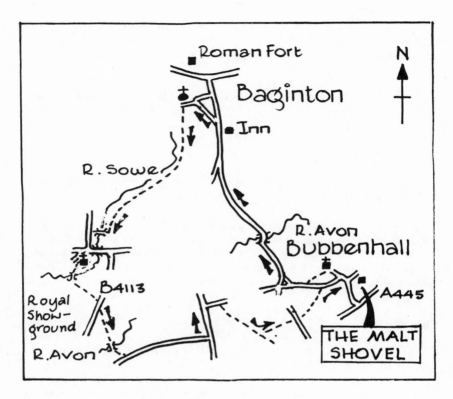

of the church) to cross the bridge over the river Sowe again. There is
a sharp climb out of the valley; the path is clear through farmland to
the B4113. Turn right then left after a few steps at a signed path. We
are now on the Centenary Way, a long distance route through
Warwickshire.

Take the signed direction over a large field. The path crosses the
Avon and a vehicle drive. Follow the path to a lane at the hamlet of
Stareton. Turn left along the road then left again at a T-junction. Take
the first lane right. Within 300 yards a path is signed on the right.

Go across a footbridge and climb a stile to a field. There are more
Centenary Way waymarks to lead us at the edge of fields then left to
a lane emerging to the left of a farm. Cross directly over (still on the
Centenary Way).

Within a few steps climb a stile right then resume the old heading
(with hedge to the left). There is soon another stile to take us back to
the original field. A further stile shows the way then keep this
direction to a lane. Bubbenhall and the Malt Shovel are to the right.

㉙ Ullenhall
The Winged Spur

This pub has a rather rare name and is said to be the only one so-named in England. To find the origin we have to go back to a previous name: it was once the Catherlow Arms and the Winged Spur was the coat of arms of the Knight family. The Knights had been associated with Ullenhall village since 1554 and they reached the pinnacle of their glory when Robert Knight was granted the title of Earl of Catherlow Viscount Barrells of Barrells Park.

Today Ullenhall has lost all its shops and the Winged Spur is a focal point of the village. There is one large bar where the beers sold are Boddingtons, Flowers and a guest beer. When I called it was Morland Speckled Hen. There is a good choice of lagers and draught Strongbow for cider drinkers.

There is a modest but very reasonably-priced menu of standard fare with an especially tasty home-made steak and kidney pie. There is nothing specific for vegetarians but they will find choices to suit them. The opening hours are standard pub hours both weekdays and Sundays and outdoor customers have plenty of benches and tables. This is a pub where well-behaved children and dogs are welcomed into the pub.

Telephone: 01564 792005.

How to get there: Ullenhall is just off the A4189 between Henley-in-Arden and Redditch. The Winged Spur is in the centre of the village.

Parking: There is a car park at the rear of the pub.

Length of the walk: 7 miles. Map: OS Landranger series 150 Worcester and 139 Birmingham (inn GR 122675).

There is a mainly pastoral landscape on this walk. The route passes St Mary's church, Ullenhall. This is the 'new' St Mary's from the last century. The old St Mary's is across the fields to the east; only the nave remains. The rather notorious Lady Luxborough is buried here.

The Walk

Opposite the pub a path is signed at the side of new houses. Cross a sheep pasture along a clear path to a lane by the church. Turn right a few steps then climb a stile on the right. Turn left then at once climb another stile to a meadow. Take the arrowed direction across the field to a step stile.

Beyond the stile walk to another then alongside a left-hand hedge. Over a far corner stile regain the old heading but with the border of the field now on the right side. Keep this direction until just over a plank bridge. Turn left to a road. Turn right for 300 yards. By a farm drive go over a stile on the right. In a pasture continue near the right-hand edge to cross a stony drive of a house.

In the following rough pasture make for the footbridge in the far right corner then continue over a rough fence stile. Maintain the heading passing just to the right of old brick animal shelters to go through a gateway (gate may be missing). Walk by the right-hand bushy hedge to a far stile and similar in the next field. Keep the direction to go through a corner metal gate.

There is now a large elongated field. Walk the length to the stile in the distant right-hand corner. Ahead pass through the gateway of a hedge (no gate) to a corner stile (well to the right of a rather elegant bungalow). Follow the arrowed way to a road. Turn left.

Just past a row of cottages climb a stile on the left. In the meadow walk alongside the left-hand wood to a far corner stile. Continue to a lane. Turn left then left again down the drive of a school. Follow the drive past the school (on right) and farm (on left) along a wide rough farm track which twists and turns.

When a concrete way is reached swing left to pass Lower Skilts Farms. There are some very ancient buildings here – note the old doorways and windows. Keep ahead past the house and farm buildings to pick up the left-hand side of a hedge in the field beyond.

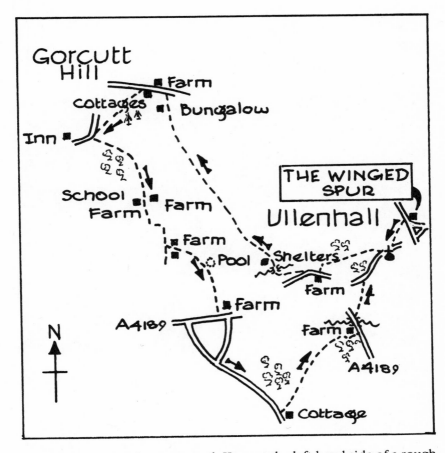

Climb a rough stile near a pool. Keep at the left-hand side of a rough pasture. Near a farm keep just to the right of brick animal shelters to a stile to a farm drive and a road. Turn left then right along a lane. Drop down to a crossroads. Turn left. Within ¾ mile and just before a cottage take a signed path on the left.

Keep near the right-hand side of the pasture for 200 yards. Climb a stile then regain the old heading (now by a left-hand hedge). Go through a far metal gate. The path is waymarked by a wire fence then (beyond a metal gate) beside a wood. Near the end of the field swing right then left through a metal gate. Continue to a road.

Turn left for 250 yards. There is a faint path through the bushes on the right to a stile to a meadow. Walk slightly left of the arrowed direction to a stile to a lane. Turn right to pick up the outward route past the 'new' church to the Winged Spur.

30 Great Alne
The Mother Huff Cap

What a strange name for a pub! To explain I think it best to quote from the poem on the menu card:

> Twix Michaelmas and Martinmas – old dame began
>   to brew;
> First she brewed some old beer – then she brewed
>   some new.
> The first to pour was cloudy beer
> But the next there came the crystal clear;
> Then she brewed a lot like that
> And on top was Huff the Cap.

The pub dates from the 16th century and is wonderfully full of atmosphere, tastefully mixing old charm with modern comfort. A tithe barn has been painstakingly transferred from a farm site to make a fine additional room (which can accommodate a bowling alley) for the pub.

A wide range of meals and snacks are served from a detailed menu – the salads are especially good 'with at least ten salad items on each

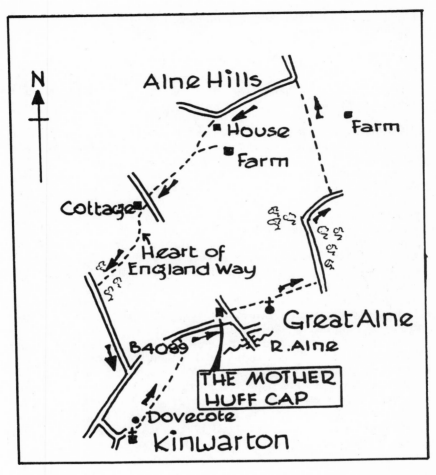

meal'. The choice is made even more difficult as there is always a specials of the day board and plenty of dishes for vegetarians. There are mini meals for toddlers but this really is a pub to return to after the walk with a good appetite.

The beers on offer at this Whitbread's house include the full range from Flowers brewery and in addition many foreign ales are offered to satisfy the current tastes. Strongbow cider is on draught. Children are allowed in the lounge and dogs have been seen to creep into the bar. Hours of opening are 11 am to 2.30 pm and 7 pm to 11 pm Monday to Saturday and the normal Sunday hours apply.

Telephone: 01789 488312.

How to get there: Great Alne is 2 miles east of Alcester on the B4089. The pub is at a junction on entering the village.

Parking: There is a car park at the side of the pub.

Length of the walk: 5 miles. Map: OS Landranger series 150 Worcester (inn GR 113593).

The Alne Hills are delightful gentle uplands with some pretty views. The route is partly along the long distance path called the Heart of England Way then goes to Kinwarton. There is little at this tiny village except a humble church with a little wooden tower and a farmstead or two. But it does possess a real gem — the 600 year old dovecote which is now in the care of the National Trust.

The Walk
There is a lane beside the pub. Opposite a footpath is signed. Keep ahead along the well-used track which runs near Great Alne's church. Keep a constant heading to emerge on a lane. Turn left. The narrow way twists sharply right. Stay on the lane but within 250 yards take a signed path up the bank left.

In the field keep alongside the left-hand border. Keep ahead through the fields on a constant heading to a lane. Turn left. After almost ½ mile take a signed path over a stile left, alongside a house drive. Take the arrowed route to join a farm drive to a lane. Turn left then at once right along a signed path which passes by a cottage.

Now on the Heart of England Way follow the waymarked route to a lane. Turn left to the B4089. Turn right then left after ¼ mile to Kinwarton. Bear left when the lane divides to go by the church. At the end of the lane keep ahead to walk just to the right of the dovecote. Keep ahead then bear left to the B4089. Great Alne and the Mother Huff Cap are to the right.